Preaching
Mark's
Unsettling
Messiah

Preaching
Mark's
Unsettling
Messiah

DAVID FLEER / DAVE BLAND, EDS.

CHALICE
PRESS

ST. LOUIS, MISSOURI

Cover art: Wall painting, Crosier Monastery, Louvain, Belgium;
    Photograph © Crosiers
Cover and interior design: Elizabeth Wright

Visit Chalice Press on the World Wide Web at
www.chalicepress.com

10 9 8 7 6 5 4 3 2 1   06 07 08 09 10

Library of Congress Cataloging–in–Publication Data

Preaching Mark's unsettling Messiah / David Fleer and Dave Bland, editors.
    p. cm.
Includes bibliographical references.
ISBN-13: 978-0-8272-2986-0 (pbk.)
ISBN-10: 0-8272-2986-0 (pbk.)
1. Bible. N.T. Mark—Homiletical use. 2. Bible. N.T. Mark—Criticism, interpretation, etc. 3. Jesus Christ—Person and offices—Biblical teaching. I. Fleer, David. II. Bland, Dave.
BS2585.55.P74 2006
226.3'06—dc22

2005037541

Printed in the United States of America

Royce Dickinson Jr.'s life reflected the presence of God and was evidence of one who lived in the world imagined in scripture. Royce recently expressed his thoughts on preaching and reality. Listen, and you will hear Royce's characteristic reflection, insight, and robust energy:

> Over the years, my preaching has become more "confessional" in nature. I subscribe to what I sometimes call "Jacob Preaching": when you wrestle with the text all week, don't be surprised if you're limping on Sunday! I am on a never-ending journey to knowing. Does this make sense? I want to be an example of someone who hungers and thirsts to know God, who is driven over and over again to the text, for in it is a word from God. And I know such a endeavor is painful!

Royce lived with a deep passion to grow in and be changed by God. He was a man of wisdom, integrity, honesty, and keen wit. He ministered with the love of Christ. Playing a pivotal role in the Sermon Seminar since its inception, Royce's scholarship encouraged us to engage world-class scholars, while his delightful personality refreshed us all. His absence leaves a painful and irreplaceable void.

It is altogether appropriate that we dedicate this volume to the memory of our beloved colleague and friend, Royce Dickinson Jr. (1956–2005).

Contents

Contributors

FREDERICK D. AQUINO is professor of systematic theology in the Graduate School of Theology at Abilene Christian University. He has team-taught courses on preaching and theology. Recent publications include *Communities of Informed Judgment: Newman's Illative Sense and Accounts of Rationality* (Catholic University of America Press, 2004) and *Unveiling Glory,* coauthored with Jeff Childers (ACU Press, 2004). He has published articles in *Restoration Quarterly, Downside Review, Newman Studies Journal, Christian Higher Education,* and *Louvain Studies*. Frederick and his wife, Michelle, have a six-year-old son, David, and a two-year-old daughter, Elizabeth.

JOHN BARTON has been involved in preaching and Christian ministry for sixteen years. He first preached for three years at the New Hope Church of Christ in Brownsville, Tennessee, while completing his M.Div. at Harding University Graduate School of Religion. After that, John and his wife, Sara, served with a mission team in Uganda, East Africa, from 1994 to 2002. There, John earned his Ph.D. in African Philosophy (Makerere University). Since 2002, John has been professor of philosophy at Rochester College in Rochester Hills, Michigan, also preaching regularly in congregations. John has a passion for exploring the intersections of faith and culture, as well as for integrating incarnational ministry with responsible proclamation.

CHRIS BENJAMIN earned his M.Div. and D.Min. from Abilene Christian University and preached for the Lake Jackson Church of Christ in southeast Texas. He now preaches for the West-Ark Church of Christ in Fort Smith, Arkansas.

DAVE BLAND preached for the Eastside Church of Christ in Portland, Oregon, before coming to the White Station congregation in Memphis. Dave earned his Ph.D. in rhetoric at the University of Washington and has long cultivated an interest in wisdom literature. Dave also serves as professor of homiletics at Harding University Graduate School of Religion in Memphis.

FRED B. CRADDOCK has been a preacher, a teacher of preaching, and a writer on the subject of preaching for all his professional life and well into his retirement. With his Ph.D. in New Testament

(Vanderbilt), Fred has understood the sermon as the future of the biblical text. Long identified with the "New Homiletic," Fred's more notable publications include *Preaching, Overhearing the Gospel,* and *As One Without Authority.*

DAVID FLEER enjoyed a long-tenured pulpit ministry with the Vancouver Church of Christ in the state of Washington. His Ph.D. in speech communication from the University of Washington moved him into teaching at Rochester College, where he is currently professor of religion and communication and vice president of church relations.

MARK FROST has been the preaching minister since 1978 for the Church of Christ in Trenton, Michigan, where he also serves as an elder. He holds a bachelor's degree from Harding University and a master's degree from Cincinnati Bible Seminary, with additional graduate studies at the Harding Graduate School of Religion and Ashland Theological Seminary.

SPENCER FURBY is the minister for Slicer Street Church of Christ in Kennett, Missouri. Spencer first studied preaching at Crowley's Ridge College and then at Freed Hardeman University and the Doctor of Ministry program at Harding University Graduate School.

MARK HENDERSON preached the word of God for congregations in Austin and Boulder before moving to Oklahoma City, where he has served the Quail Springs Church of Christ since 1999. He received his M.Div. in 1991 and a D.Min. in 2004 from Abilene Christian University.

MORNA D. HOOKER is a New Testament scholar, who for twenty-two years was Lady Margaret's Professor in the University of Cambridge. Before that, she taught at King's College in London and the University of Oxford. Now "retired," she continues to write, lecture, teach, and edit. Morna has written many books, including a *Commentary on St. Mark, Beginnings: Keys that Open the Gospels,* and *Endings: Invitations to Discipleship.* For many years she was joint editor of *The Journal of Theological Studies.* She is a Methodist Local Preacher and one of a small group responsible for translating the New Testament for *The Revised English Bible.*

DAVID KELLER holds a D.Min. degree from Harding University Graduate School and has preached for congregations in Mississippi, Pennsylvania, Delaware, and West Virginia. For over thirty years, he taught Bible and ministry courses at Northeastern Christian

Junior College and Ohio Valley University. He currently teaches ministry and communication courses at Rochester College.

MARK LOVE has earned M.A. and D.Min. degrees from Abilene Christian University, and received his M.Div. from Pepperdine University. Mark served the East County Church of Christ in Gresham, Oregon, as Minister of the Word for eleven years before accepting his current position as assistant professor of ministry and director of ministry events at ACU.

ROBERT STEPHEN REID was senior pastor of two congregations and a long-term interim pastor of three others while earning his M.A. and Ph.D. in rhetoric from the University of Washington. He received his M.Div. from Fuller Theological Seminary. Bob is chair of the rhetoric division of the Academy of Homiletics, writes books on preaching, preaches whenever the pastor is gone at First Baptist Church of Dubuque, and oversees the Master of Arts in the Communication Program at the University of Dubuque.

JERRY ANDREW TAYLOR started preaching at the age of fourteen. While still in college, he preached for the Ardis Street Church of Christ in Sulphur Springs, Texas. He has served as the lead minister in churches in Texas, North Carolina, and Georgia. He received his M.Div. and D.Min. from Perkins School of Theology, Southern Methodist University in Dallas, Texas. He serves as a Bible professor at Abilene Christian University and the associate preaching minister at the Highland Church of Christ in Abilene, Texas.

RICHARD F. WARD is an associate professor of preaching and performance studies at the Iliff School of Theology in Denver, Colorado, where he teaches courses in storytelling, performance of biblical texts, and drama. Ordained with the United Church of Christ, he has served churches in the United Methodist Church and the Church of the Brethren. Richard has also held the Clement-Muehl Chair in Communication Arts at Yale Divinity School and was assistant professor of speech communication at the Candler School of Theology.

JOHN YORK has served since the fall of 2000 as one of the preaching ministers for the Woodmont Hills Church in Nashville, Tennessee. Previously he was preaching minister for churches in Oregon, Tennessee, and Texas, and taught in colleges and universities in Oregon and Tennessee. He completed a Ph.D. in New Testament at Emory University and has been professor of Bible and preaching at Lipscomb University since 1998.

Preaching Mark's Unsettling Messiah

DAVID FLEER AND DAVE BLAND

Framing the Essential

We have our ways for claiming that something possesses great value. We raise our voice or whisper for conversational emphasis. With e-mail we may capitalize all letters, or underline or italicize a word if possible. When studying, we highlight a sentence or create a marginal asterisk to signal an essential thought. We expect the suspense novel to save until the final chapter the critical details necessary to solve the mystery. In scripture, authors employ creative methods to convey the "most important matters." Jesus speaks plainly to the Pharisees, contrasting their spice tithing against "the weightier matters of the law" (Mt. 23:23). Paul is just as clear when he informs the Corinthians that Jesus' death, burial, resurrection, and appearances are of first importance" (1 Cor. 15:3). In a dramatic courtroom setting, Micah claims that God's requirements are justice, kindness, and humility (Mic. 6:8). "Weightier," "most important," and "what the Lord requires" are direct and clear. At times, however, the signals in scripture are indirect and subtle.

Fred Craddock is one of the first in our era to point to the indirection of scripture as a paradigm for preaching. The "founder of the New Homiletic"[1] opens this volume with the sermon "Jesus

1

Deeply Grieved." The sermon models preaching's essential qualities and is a brilliant example of inductive form, saving until the final sentence the long-awaited resolution to the sermon's generated concern. More critically, Craddock's sermon vividly demonstrates the importance of going to the text and staying in the text long enough for meaning to surface. In other words, Craddock honors Mark's ability to "preach."

As Craddock's sermon reflects, Mark's gospel signals important matters through indirection and subtle arrangement. Consider, for example, how Mark uses an *inclusio* (more memorably termed a "sandwich") to feature an essential teaching. Mark starts a story, pauses to tell another story in its entirety, and then returns to the former tale to bring it to completion. Mark's gospel employs this A, B, A' pattern with some frequency, creating a frame for dynamic juxtapositions that allow listeners to experience essential material. So when Jesus' family hears of his threatening work schedule, they move to "restrain him" (3:20–21). Mark then stalls the familial movement to deliver another fully packaged tale, eventually turning attention back to the arriving family (3:31–32). This *inclusio* allows Mark to highlight Jesus' stunning revelation, "Who are my mother and my brothers…Whoever does the will of God is my brother and sister and mother" (3:33, 35).

Or consider Mark's tale of the fig tree. Matthew has the temple's cleansing precede the simultaneous cursing and withering of the tree.[2] Mark separates the cause and effect. He positions the temple cleansing between the two, thus turning the outcast religious profiteers into the sandwich's "meat." Mark's arrangement of cursing, cleansing, and withering sets up Jesus' teaching. Mark frames corrupt religion practiced in the temple and symbolized by the fig tree's demise to create a hearing for the "most important" teaching that follows. Jesus' religion, which fills the void left by the excised corruption, is summed up in three words: faith, prayer, and forgiveness.[3] Mark's content and form are entwined to effectively present "the essentials."

Following Mark's lead, the means to live in the text's drama is to ensure that the imagined world remain 3D in its arrangement, style, and content. Many exegetical sermons unwittingly objectify the biblical world into a distant, dusty, and boring land. Mark's sermon is full of life. Craddock finds fault with the minister who assumes audience familiarity with the biblical narrative and thus jettisons important details from its story.[4] This pulpit attitude says, "If you will be patient and sit through the biblical stuff, I promise to tell you very soon now the interesting story about Uncle Clyde surviving a plane crash."[5] What makes Mark's sermon so engaging are its nuanced and multidimensional narrative qualities and its stealth ability to highlight the most critical features. What then might we learn from Mark's preaching as we find our own voice?

Preaching's Model

When defining a "sermon," congregations, preachers, biblical scholars, and rhetoricians all seem to underscore different aspects. The audience, text, or the preacher each finds emphasis from different quarters. Craddock weaves audience, text, preacher, and God into a tapestry, teaching us to ask, "Does the sermon say and do what the biblical text says and does?" Be mindful that it is far more important "to get it heard than to get it said." A lithe sage[6] to whom the vulnerable preacher looks for encouragement and advice, Craddock urges us to do the most difficult thing in the world: "say something important in public." He understands that "the central sacrament of the human body is to speak" and draws his own breath in pain to tell the gospel story. The sermon, like the poem, is a "fragile craft…winged for the heart."[7]

Craddock observes the details of our common lives while deftly handling the biblical text. Yet his autobiographical account of how he came to preach (in a style he likens to "playing the piccolo"), where he moved upon retirement, and with whom he now works is a profoundly humble story. The irony, of course, is that we often perceive Craddock's skills to be beyond the reach of mere mortals such as ourselves, knowing that "David does not fit well into Saul's armor." Yet Craddock claims that his style of preaching was born in an effort to compensate for his *inadequacies* (his voice and physical stature). After a childhood engaged in story, enhanced by formal training in New Testament, Craddock eventually found narrative preaching embedded in the gospels.

Craddock's model is the gospel writer, Mark, whom we consider the *preacher*. So, the essays and sermons in this volume do not treat Mark as a sermonic resource or a storehouse of viable preaching pericopes. Rather, we look to Mark to see what Mark is looking at. Mark is the first Christian preacher, and his gospel the first sermon.

This Volume's Movement

This book is divided into halves that depend on each other. The heart of the book's opening section is Fred Craddock's sermon and his guiding essay. The other chapters in this portion add to Craddock's insights by incorporating the biblical studies of Morna Hooker, the theological work of Frederick Aquino, the performance studies of Richard Ward, and the cultural perspective of John Barton. They provide a wide scope of substantive Markan scholarship designed specifically for preachers.

Morna Hooker's elegant chapters work on one presupposition: How literature begins and ends is important. Once something is set in motion, it is critical to know how to come to a stop. "You cannot simply jump out of a moving vehicle." Hooker searches for literary clues, helping her readers ask reasonable literary questions of Mark's gospel. Attentive to Mark's beginnings and endings, readers (or hearers) wish to step into the plot and sort things out. Both chapters move beyond Hooker's prior focus on the *distinctives* of Mark's opening and closing lines[8] to the *links* from which these two sections connect to the entirety of Mark's gospel. Hooker's work deepens our hearing and exploration skills and stimulates imaginative connections with the gospel's language and plot.

Fred Aquino reverses Mark's inquiry, "Who is Jesus?" to ask, "What does it mean to be fully human in this gospel's narrative?" He guides us through Mark's disruption of the familiar into a new way of being in the world. He tracks the logic of God's kingdom through the rhetoric of irony, the dialectic of sight and blindedness, and the expansion of the borders of human self-understanding.

John Barton creates a roundtable discussion of Mel Gibson's *The Passion of the Christ*, with preachers, Gibson's critics and fans, and Mark, centered on the probing question, "What perspective would Mark offer to help us further evaluate Gibson's film and our Christian experience?" Arguing that preaching converses with the influences and powers that impact our lives, Barton notes Mark's distance from Gibson's artistic expressions, extra biblical sources, *and* our Sunday worship experience. Mark's concern, he concludes, is not the brutality of Jesus' suffering, but *who* endured this suffering and *why*. Judging the film to be dependent on a "convoluted mixture of the four gospels" and extra biblical material, Barton asks Mark to question us, "Are *we* guilty of creating a Jesus in our own image?"

Richard Ward claims that Mark's gospel read aloud has the possibility to release the story to speak in new ways. Ward provides clues to how Mark might preach and perform in our time. Through sound, attitude, gesture, and intention, the preacher's authenticity arises out of an experiential knowledge of Mark's gospel and draws on one's deepest emotional and intellectual investment to become the "embodied presence" of the author, Mark. Fred Craddock recently said that if he were to start over in ministry he'd find within the congregation five persons who read well and "get them training," so important is the public reading of scripture.[9] Ward's thoughtful chapter is the place to begin.

The book's second half provides sample sermons from specific texts that incorporate the theoretical underpinnings of the book's first section. The essays and sermons are bound together by (1) Fred Craddock's opening sermon, which models the book's theme and suggested characteristics; (2) sermon introductions that deductively connect that specific sermon with the book's early chapters; (3) each sermon's inductive application of the essays' suggestions; and (4) the response, in sermon and essay, to the same questions: "How can we draw our congregations into the world Mark has imagined, and how might we proclaim the gospel as Mark?"

Using Professor Hooker's material, Jerry Taylor's sermon, delivered before a congregation of preachers at the seminar, is richly textured with African American typology and effective stylistic repetition. Most of these sermons were preached after the 2005 seminar, with attention to the opening essays and Craddock's "Jesus Deeply Grieved." Each sermon is a fine example of praxis *and* theory created in the world Mark imagines.

Preaching Mark's Unsettling Messiah grew out of the May 2005 Rochester College Sermon Seminar, when over two hundred ministers from thirty-two states or provinces, representing twenty identifiable Christian fellowships, convened a conference on preaching and the gospel of Mark. This vibrant gathering united Evangelical and Mainline[10] preachers by moving them into the world Mark's gospel imagines. We became "the unity of all believers in the pursuit of scripture," an ecumenicity that nourishes and disciplines us to preach to the people to whom God calls us. This volume intends to expand the seminar's harmony and immersion in the Markan world. Our deepest desire is that this book will be a viable tool for this reforming center of Christianity, providing a workable resource for preaching the Messiah Mark proclaims.

PART ONE

Essays on Mark

Jesus Deeply Grieved[1]

Mark 14:32–42

FRED B. CRADDOCK

I read the story in Mark as though I were there. And I was, thanks to Mark. Mark gives me and other readers of his gospel the extraordinary advantage of being in on events and conversations that otherwise were totally private. When Jesus was baptized, the voice from heaven said, "You are my Son." It was a voice directed to Jesus. The crowd around there didn't hear the voice, apparently. As far as I know, the only ones to hear it are Jesus...and you. He took Peter, James, and John up onto the Mount of Transfiguration. Jesus was transfigured before them. Just the four of them experiencing glory denied the nine disciples left at the foot of the mountain. Just the four of them up there: Jesus, Peter, James, and John. Well, actually five, with the reader, who saw it and heard it. In Gethsemane, Jesus lies prostrate on the ground with his disciples all asleep, except Judas...and you. We are there, as the readers. We see him, and we hear him. What an extraordinary advantage we readers have in the gospel of Mark, experiencing what the sleeping apostles miss altogether.

I don't much like this advantage. It puts me in an awkward position, partially because I am uncomfortable being party to these otherwise private moments. I don't appreciate very much this special seat. I don't have the credentials to be here and hear and see this. Who does not rather feel a stranger in this world of Jesus— an intruder, whose pounding heart says, "You have no right to be here."

I don't much like this advantage because, once experienced, it easily breeds pride: "If I'd been there, I wouldn't have been asleep. He could have counted on me to stay awake right there beside him while he suffered."

And that pride can breed a judgmental spirit: "To sleep through their Lord's agony is inexcusable and unforgivable." I must confess that much of my early preaching was from this vantage point. And hardly a character around Jesus was spared my sword. "What's the matter with those people?" I was the reader, and I was on the inside.

Let there be no doubt, we readers have an advantage. The advantage to the mind is obvious; we can understand what characters in the story cannot. The advantage to the heart is obvious; being there, being present to what is said and done, has powerful affective impact.

And so they slept while we heard and saw everything. Actually, I am glad they were asleep. Better asleep than out engaged in mischief contrary to all Jesus had taught and they had vowed to follow. I don't trust Simon Peter to be awake. He'd be out some- where among the opposition, overestimating the strength of his loyalty, only to cave under pressure: "I never in my life met this Jesus." And James and John, you can't trust them to be awake, in town getting matching sweatshirts printed front and back, "We are Number One." It's best they sleep. Of the twelve, only Judas is awake; and he is out making a deal for thirty pieces of silver. I wish *he* were asleep.

Actually, the reason I am glad they are asleep is that they couldn't bear to see him like this. I do not refer to the arrival of the crowd that seized Jesus. The disciples were all awake for that, and what did they do? "All of them deserted him and fled" (14:50). No, I refer to the emotionally and intellectually demanding hours preceding the arrest, during which their Lord and Christ lay on the ground, agitated, distressed, and deeply grieved. Who is this, prostrate in the dirt?

In those bright spring days in Galilee his deeds of power persuaded them. He was a healer in Galilee. People could just touch his clothes, and all manner of diseases were healed. Not even a legion of demons could withstand the force of his word. Even the winds and the waves obeyed him. He was powerful in Galilee. But not here, not now, not this.

Later on, their memories could call up Isaiah 53, "a man of sorrows, and acquainted with grief" (53:3, KJV). Later on, they could look back and recall the psalms of lament, "Why are you cast down, O my soul, and why are you disquieted within me?" (Pss. 42, 43, and 55). Later on, they would reflect and make the connections. But not now. I think I am fair in saying that not one of them could have pointed to the man coming to pieces on the ground and declare, "This is the Messiah." I don't think one of them would think of Jesus, throwing himself on the ground, and say of him, "Behold the Son of God."

"Sit here with me. Watch. Pray. I'm so sad I could die."

Soon his voice will stir them, and they will wake. Two questions will form immediately in their minds. Both are embarrassing, but they must be asked. They are afraid to ask him; and so they ask us, the readers who have been awake through the entire account.

Question one, "What happened while we slept?" What should we say in response? We are Christians and have a pastor's heart. We don't want these sleeping disciples to feel any more guilty than they already are. That's not what we are to do, beat them down and stomp on them. No. Something uplifting and encouraging is needed.

We know other accounts of what happened in Gethsemane, so why not answer their question with the account that strikes the softest blow. Perhaps that would be the gospel of John. After all, in John the experience of Jesus most like "Gethsemane" occurs earlier at the tomb of Lazarus (Jn. 11), where Jesus weeps and is deeply troubled, "Where have you laid him?" (v. 34). Again, in chapter 12, Jesus struggles. With a disturbed spirit, he expresses the crisis: "What shall I say, 'Father, make me an exception to the rule that death is necessary for life?'" (v. 27 paraphrased). But his embrace of God's will is complete; he will be lifted up on the cross and, through the cross, to God. Therefore, when Jesus arrives at "Gethsemane,"[2] he speaks as one for whom the crisis is past, as one who has walked to the edge, faced death, and returned free. Hence, there is no agony, no groaning, no beating the breast. In fact, John called Gethsemane "a garden." The rest of John is as smooth as a beatitude. He talks about the coming of the Holy Spirit, how he'll be with them always. It is so comforting. John certainly offers a gentle answer to the disciples' question.

But so would Luke. In Luke, Jesus kneels in prayer, not throwing himself on the ground. Luke's account is no black and white photo with jagged edges; it is, rather, a portrait. You can hang it over your couch and invite friends in and nibble at cheese and crackers and sip wine and talk about what a beautiful painting this is. No wonder most churches have at least one window with Jesus in Gethsemane. The light is on his face. He is intentional, kneeling. Not hours rolling on the ground. In fact, had not later scribes added sweating drops of blood (22:43–44), there would be no sense of Jesus being in anguish. I don't blame the scribes. Here I am, myself, trying to fix it. Luke would have a gentle answer.

One could answer the question, "What happened while we slept?" with Matthew and still offer comfort as well as information. Matthew is here most like Mark, but with a most heartening addition. Once Jesus had been arrested, he says to his followers, "Do you think that I cannot appeal to my Father, and he will at once send me more than twelve legions of angels? (26:53). In other words, Jesus in Gethsemane is not a powerless victim; the apparent weakness is, in fact, restrained power. That's the title of Matthew's gospel: "He could have, but he did not." Such an understanding of what occurred would surely bring relief to the disciples.

What will we say to them when they awaken? We need to soften it someway. Perhaps we could use a line or two from Hebrews, Jesus, "who for a little while was made lower than the angels" (Heb. 2:9). That's a consoling thought. You can stand anything if it is just for a little while. It will be over soon; don't worry about it. Or we could quote, "we have one who in every respect has been tested as we are" (Heb. 4:15). He knew every pain and puzzle we face. That is why we are able to approach the throne of grace with understanding and sympathy; he knows exactly how it is. Would it be cricket for us to steal from another book to help Mark? This is tough. I used to preach like that: "Don't worry folks, I'll help you out." I'd reach around and find another verse to scotch up my demanding text.

But we must be honest with the disciples and with ourselves. We are reading Mark, and we are not to seek refuge elsewhere, however painful the lines from this evangelist. In Gethsemane Jesus throws himself on the ground, acknowledging that he is distressed and deeply grieved, even to the point of death. He seems to be going to pieces, as one suffering a breakdown. He prays for hours, reciting the creed behind all creeds—all things are possible with

God. But apparently no relief comes. What he cries from the cross is already true, "My God, my God, why have you forsaken me? I can bear the pain of my disciples sleeping, of Judas betraying, of Peter denying, but silence from you, O God, I cannot bear." Painful as it is, the disciples must be told: "This is what happened while you slept." They should not be shielded from having to deal with it.

The second question the disciples will ask when they awake is, "Will he ever forgive us?" An appropriate question. There is no need to turn the screw one more time, reminding them of their confession of faith not many weeks ago before the trip to Jerusalem, or of their pledges of loyalty at dinner this very evening. They know there is hardly a sin more serpentine, more scaly, more foul than this, to sleep while their leader lies shaking on the ground, all alone, abandoned by earth and heaven. Jesus had spoken in Galilee of a sin so heinous as to be beyond the reach of forgiving grace; have they committed that sin? The thought of it would have been too heavy to bear.

Asleep in Gethsemane; can you believe it? Asleep, while Jesus agonizes alone. A graduate student in biochemistry has finished the class work and, just last month, the comprehensive exams. Pass those, and he moves on to the dissertation; and, finally, the doctorate is his. Fail those, and it is over; he goes home. Today, at 5 p.m., the grades will be posted. It is a long day. Sweating, he approaches the bulletin board. He failed. What does he say to his parents, to his fiancé? He is totally alone. He walks the streets. Inside the houses along the streets families are eating, laughing, enjoying each other, watching TV. Suddenly he is filled with rage and begins to throw rocks at the houses, breaking windows. Later at the police station he explains: "There I was on the streets, dying inside, and those people were eating and having a good time. How could they do it? I just lost it." It makes no sense; it makes all kinds of sense. Jesus, you have every right to be outraged: you are grieved even to the point of death, and good friends are totally relaxed, fast asleep.

Longtime friends are divorcing this summer after twenty-two years of marriage. No one who knows them looks for the other woman or the other man. The obstacle between them seems immovable; at least the wife thinks so. Several years ago they lost a seven-year old daughter to cancer. The illness was long and painful and draining on everyone. The last of several hospitals, the last of many treatments was in Rochester, Minnesota, far from the family home; but no matter, the illness of their child was the center of every decision, every action, every plan. Near the hospital, they had a room in a Ronald McDonald House. They were prayed out, stressed out, worn out. The daughter's condition worsened; the doctors shook their heads, "We can only relieve her pain," they said. They sat together beside the bed waiting, trying to call up one more prayer. "I'll go to the room, get a nap, and then come and relieve you," he said. While he slept, the daughter slipped away, her frail body showing little sign of finality. She died while her father slept. That was more than a fact; it was a charge brought by his wife into divorce court. "Who can live with, who can be married to a man who sleeps while his daughter is dying? I will not, I cannot ever forgive him."

"Do you think he will ever forgive us for sleeping while he grieved so deeply, threw himself on the ground, and seemed to be coming totally apart?" the disciples will ask us, who have had the advantage of being awake through the entire ordeal. We should have permission to go back to the dinner conversation earlier that evening, "Did he not say to you at dinner this very night, 'After I am raised up, I will go ahead of you to Galilee'? Does that answer your question?" Apparently not, because they remained self-absorbed and depressed. "That was then," they say, "but this is now. Then we made bold pledges of loyalty to the death; now we have slept, leaving him to suffer alone."

We readers realize that not even the memory of everything Jesus said and did will save the disciples from self-condemnation. However encouraging such reminders might be, they will not save the disciples. Without Easter, the gospel is not fully gospel.

The real advantage we have as readers is to move ahead three days and tell them, "There is a young man in dazzling white who will say to the women at the tomb, 'You are looking for Jesus of Nazareth, who was crucified. He has been raised; he is not here. Look, there is the place they laid him. But go, tell his disciples and Peter that he is going ahead of you to Galilee; there you will see him, *just as he told you*'" (16:6–7).

"Do you think he will forgive us?"

I think he already has.

2

The New Homiletic for Latecomers

Suggestions for Preaching from Mark[1]

FRED B. CRADDOCK

I sincerely thank David Fleer and Dave Bland for inviting me to participate. This is, on their part, an exercise in memory, because I have been twelve years deep in retirement from the classroom. I live in a rural area and work with southern Appalachian people who don't read any of the books that you read. I'm working with ministers who have never been to seminary, never to college. I'm a kind of rolling store, going from community to community having workshops for these serious, committed, and highly intelligent ministers without much education. So they trust me to share what I know, and we work together on sermons. We work with the children by taking music and art and storytelling to the Head Starts, to three- and four-year-olds. I am asked once in a while by former colleagues at Emory why I haven't retired, and the plain fact is you can retire from a job or a position, but you can't retire from your ordination. So I do what I can, where I can, with what I have.

How Can a Piccolo Preach?

I entered into the arena of homiletics in a very unusual way. I was not trained in that field. My education had been in New Testament all the way to the terminal degree. Some students, when

14

I began to teach at seminary, said, "All this is fine for the classroom, but it's a long way from my pulpit."

And I said, "If you do your work carefully, you'll have something to say on Sunday."

They would write exegetical papers and make A's, but say, "This has nothing to do with helping me to preach." I got tired of hearing that, of course. So I formed a little seminar of last semester seniors. We worked together, from exegesis to sermon, but it was a very poor class. I did a poor job, because when you bring things that you do almost automatically to the surface for a critical evaluation, it's like watching your feet when you walk—you can't walk.

I asked for a year's sabbatical to Tübingen, Germany. Tübingen was a delightful experience, with great lectures in New Testament and theology; but when I talked about preaching, they said, "You should have stayed at home. People still go to church in America. We don't go to church over here. We don't know anything about preaching." Toward the end of my time there, I met retired professor Hermann Diem walking down the middle of a narrow street, the Neekar Gasse, about to be hit by a Volkswagen. I helped him over to the side of the street and told him who I was. He wanted to know what I was doing there. When I explained, he said, "You should just go home to America; this is no place for you." And then he turned to walk away—of course, I thanked him for his help. Then he stopped, looked back, and said, "Do you read Kierkegaard?" I said, "I tried it a time or two, but it was very difficult." He said, "Read Kierkegaard."

So back home, I read Kierkegaard. If you want to read Kierkegaard, though, you have to read it in the right order, or it's just a blank wall. Paul Holmer at Yale told me to read first *The Point of View of My Work as an Author*, which opens doors to the rest. It was helpful to me because I was beginning the teaching of preaching. I went back bantam roosterlike, not taking that first defeat as the final word, and taught another class on preaching some portion of the New Testament.

This occurred in the late sixties, and people weren't interested in preaching. In the late sixties, people were painting signs, marching around city hall, trying to bring down all the high places in the country and shatter all traditions in the way people dressed, the way they behaved, the way they talked. Some schools just quit offering preaching altogether. Nobody wanted to take preaching. "It's too traditional. It's too authoritative. It comes from on high, and we don't listen to voices from on high." In the middle of the radical revolution of the sixties, there I was trying to teach preaching.

The method I developed grew out of three things. First, desperation: How can I teach preaching in this atmosphere? Second, How can I teach preaching when my own style of preaching has been created out of compensations for what I don't have? I had to build detours around the fact that I had no stature and no strength of voice. When I started preaching I tried to imitate the thundering preachers who were in my home church; but they were all big, tall, loud, full of thunder and lightning. When I tried to do that, it was ridiculous. People laughed. I wasted several years trying to be a drum and a trumpet until I finally accepted the fact that I was at best a piccolo. How can a piccolo preach? I grew up in a rural area without transportation. I wasn't inside a church building until I was nine. With illness and isolation, I was terribly under-socialized. I didn't feel that I had the right to impose my manufactured and compensating efforts on people who had other gifts: trumpets and bass drums that could call for the cannon to speak to the sky, and it would do it.

Third, I also had to teach preaching that was appropriate to my own graduate study, New Testament. It was helpful for me to reflect, with the help of a few people—Lee Keck and some others—that the way you study a passage of scripture is to work with its details and toward an interpretation, a general statement of its meaning. You don't start with a statement of its meaning and then go into the details. In other words, you work inductively to do exegesis. So I thought, "If I do that with the text in the study, maybe I could do that with the text in the pulpit." And so began my own journey in the field of preaching.

About 1970, on the campus of Phillips University, Enid, Oklahoma, at a little print shop for curriculum materials, I asked if they would print this little book for me to use in my class. They said, "How many do you want?" I said, "Print fifty, and I can use it several semesters." They printed fifty copies of *As One Without Authority*. But it was poorly done—seams fell apart, didn't fit, and it was a mess. But gradually I got a better copy, and eventually, somebody else wanted to publish it.

I've always felt a bit embarrassed that *As One Without Authority* had an influence beyond my intention. I appreciated people reading it and finding value. In a sense, I was relieved, because I tried to follow the natural order of communication. As Joseph Sittler used to say, "The sermons we preach are all just alike, all structured the same way: Why is it that the preacher is the only one in town with all that symmetry?" And I tried to take advantage of the natural flow of communication. But I was afraid to try it because it didn't *seem* like preaching.

So when I preached in the church, I preached the way I was taught: introduction, announce my points, develop each point, and conclude with a summary. It was healthy enough and had some merit. But when I would be invited to a PTA or civic club to speak, I spoke in an entirely different way. After one speech to a Kiwanis group, a member of the church was present and said, "Why don't you talk to us this way at the church?"

I replied, "At the church I'm preaching."

"Couldn't you preach this way?"

It gave me the shakes, but I tried it on Sunday evening because there's nobody at church on Sunday evening but my wife and kids. Even she said, "What were you *doing*?"

I recite that beginning to tell you of the unusual birth of my approach to scripture and preaching, with elements of desperation and compensation for not having the strength of voice, size, or presence. You would expect someone like me to develop a style of preaching that might be comfortable for preachers like myself who did not go thundering into and out of the pulpit.

Epochs and the New Homiletic

David and Dave asked me to write about the New Homiletic. Those who mark eras or stages or epochs, like marking on the face of a door the growth of a child, do it with preaching. Old Homiletic, New Homiletic: there are a lot of different ways to do it.

I went not long ago to hear a national authority on generation communication. Very powerful and persuasive, she said that you must socially and chronologically locate your audience. The "Traditionals" were born in the 1920s and are dying away. They served in World War II and believe in strong families, saving money, paying cash for educating their children, going to church, and behaving.

The next generation, she explained, were born in the 1940s: the "Baby Boomers." They wanted to change everything: They found things wrong with the government, churches, and all traditions. They were radical and took over the country in strange ways. They produced a lot of beautiful music and marvelous idealism: people living in poverty for the cause and working down on the Mississippi Delta for practically nothing. It was a beautiful but strange and unraveling time.

Those born in the 1960s form "Generation X." Generation X decided they couldn't change the world, didn't want to try to change the world, and became the "Me" generation, living on preferences. "I prefer this. I don't like that. And if you ask me, I'd like a consumer-oriented church. I'm a consumer. Do the things that I like. I like certain kinds of music, I like this, I like that…Or I'll find a church that will give me what I like."

And then, the last group, born in the 1980s, she said, were the "Millennials." She reported, strangely enough, "They're beginning to respect the values of grandma and grandpa. They relate very well to old people. We don't know yet what they'll turn out to be because they're still in school, but we're hopeful."

There was a question and answer time. I said, "Suppose you get up to speak, and you've got some of all four generations in the house?" She said, "You must choose one generation because you can't address all of them." Is that true? I think she's wrong. I didn't tell her that; she was a nice lady and answered my questions. But I think it is possible to preach at a level at which there is deep resonance with the truth, to prepare a sermon for people in their eighties *and* people in their teens and have each think you prepared the sermon for *them*. But if the sermon is filled with surface stuff and jargon, neither will be touched.

When you present the gospel, there exists something people recognize. Some call this forgotten truth or primordial truth. Rudolph Bultmann once said, "There is in all of us a faint recollection of the garden of Eden."Even those who hear it for the first time recognize it. I'm not silenced by this woman's thoughtful analysis of generation communication.

Those who mark eras sometimes do things like that. The old rhetoric, the new rhetoric, the old homiletic, the new homiletic. I used the term "New Homiletic" a time or two when it came out, and then I regretted it because I didn't know what I was talking about. What is *New Homiletic*? David Buttrick, now retired from Vanderbilt, likes the term; and so do some other homileticians, but what makes me nervous is that it is frequently associated with my preaching as a *new* homiletic. My preaching is hardly new. The primary mentor for my style was Søren Kierkegaard, who lived in the 1840s. So I'm a little hesitant about any claim to being one of the figures in a "*New* Homiletic."

Our descriptive terms are not always helpful. I'm now invited to speak to the postmodern time, the postmodern era. Is the pulpit going to continue to function now that we're in the postmodern era? I've been inquiring about what that means. I've gone to the philosophers because the term *postmodern* was used first in French philosophy, but the philosophers I talked to said, "Well, we don't find it a very meaningful term. It's used a good bit by linguistics; it's used by homileticians; it's used by others; but we don't really find it a useful term." They told me the phrase is used to talk about today's mind-set. For instance, one young philosopher said, "To me what it means is 'a generation of people who have no meta-narrative; that is, they have no overarching narrative. There is no story from creation to eschaton. There is only my story. It's not set in any larger story." I don't know. He said it was a characteristic of our time.

A physicist at Princeton said, "I think it means being more open to mystery." A number of homileticians said, "I think it refers to the authority of experience over tradition. Tradition no longer has the authority. Experience has the authority." A good bit of preaching believes that.

I heard a very bright, articulate woman preach not too long ago. She said, "You know all that stuff you were taught in Sunday school? Forget it." And she didn't give me time to forget it; she went on to other things I was supposed to forget. I was to forget my baptism; I was to forget the teaching I had prior to my baptism; I was to forget what I'd been taught about the Bible—"Forget all that." She said, "The only thing that matters is being present with each other." Well, I appreciated the point she was trying to make, to bring your religion up to date, to make it apply to human relationships. Good point. But she didn't have to chop down the family tree to make that point. I talked to her about it later and said, "I don't think you believe what you said." And she asked, "What are you talking about?" I told her what she said, and she claimed, "Well, I didn't really mean it that way." I said, "That's what you said."

A lot of times we do that in preaching: The diamond looks brighter if cast on a piece of black velvet. If you knock down something, then what you stand for may look better. So she told me she didn't really mean it that way; it was a case of the triumph of experience over tradition.

In the Atlanta airport, I was engaged in conversation with a retired machinist who still had the grit and grime under and around the edges of his fingernails. He was an interesting 86- or 87-year-old man. We went to our gate waiting for a plane. Into the chairs facing us came three men, and they were almost immediately in our face. They were all excited. They had been to something that had them turned on. They had fire in their minds and hearts. This old machinist and I were talking, and one of those men said, "You want to say a good word for the Lord?"

The machinist responded, "We're engaged in a conversation. Let us get through what we're talking about, and then we will talk with you."

And in a moment, another of the three said, "Don't you have anything to say for Jesus?"

I was about to respond, but the machinist beat me to it—he said, "When we finish our conversation, we'll talk to you."

The third one said, "Speak up now, or burn up later!"

Well...*that* got to us.

So the machinist said, "Are you asking me if I believe? if I'm a Christian?"

"Yes, yes, yes!" they said.

"Well," he said, "Here's what I believe: I believe in God the Father, Almighty, Maker of heaven and earth, and in Jesus Christ, his only son, our Lord, who was conceived by the Holy Spirit, born of the virgin Mary, suffered under Pontius Pilate—

At that point, one of the other men said, "We don't mean all that stuff."

The machinist said, "What do you mean?"

"What has Jesus done for you today?" And so he shared with us an experience he had had with God. Some people say the post-modern mind-set puts down the passing along of tradition and puts an accent on what's happening to a person *today*. I don't know if that's postmodern or not.

The best answer I could get as to what *postmodern* means was from a philosopher at Cornell University. This fellow was on Christmas break in Cherry Log, where I live. We spoke. He said, "The term is only meaningful to use in the way that the linguists do."

I said, "How is that?"

"All you really have is yourself and the text. That's all there is. You don't have the background; you don't have the foreground; you don't have the writer's intention; you just have the text. You read the text; you listen to the text—that's it. That's where we are now." That's an interesting observation. Whether you call it postmodern, or new hermeneutic, or new rhetoric, or whatever, that's an interesting observation, because that's exactly where I came to be at the end of the 1960s: "Here's the text."

Mark Preaches

I thought of the text in a new way. Scripture, such as Mark, ceased to be for me raw material for sermons—like bread dough which you mix, then roll it and flatten it out, and then cut out biscuits or cookies. Scripture for me had been a mass of material from which to cut out sermons. "This would make a good sermon. This piece would be a good sermon." My *new* thinking was, "Think of Mark, not as the raw material for sermons, but as the preacher. Instead of preaching Mark, Mark preaches." I discovered that I was going back to where I had been led long ago: *just listening to the text.* May I suggest, let Mark say what Mark wants to say. Let him say it. Mark was an effective communicator. After all, Mark made it into the Bible. None of my sermons are in the Bible.[2]

Mark is, as far as I know, the first effort at narrative christology. The first efforts at christology that we know of are those from Paul. Paul's christology, sometimes called epistolary christology (I call it punctiliar christology), is a completely different paradigm. Paul says, "Death, burial, resurrection. This is of first importance. This is what I received. I pass it along to you. Christ died for our sins, was buried, and rose on the third day, according to the scriptures" (1 Cor. 15:3–4 paraphrased). That's it. That was the governing paradigm whenever he spoke, sang, or worshiped. That was it. The consistency of that pattern in his life is to me a most remarkable thing. He said it many different ways: "He made him to be sin who knew no sin so that in him we might become the righteousness of God" (2 Cor. 5:21). The one who was rich became poor that by his poverty we might be rich (2 Cor. 8:9). It's the pattern of *descend, ascend; death, burial, resurrection.* Paul liturgized it: What is baptism? We're buried with Christ in baptism. The Lord's table—what is it? The death, resurrection, eternal life of Jesus Christ. Paul's own life—what was it? "I have been crucified with Christ. I bear the stigmata of Jesus. I have been crucified to the world. (Gal. 2:20 paraphrased). He thought it, he said it, he lived it, he sang it! Death, burial, resurrection: That is the gospel according to Paul.

Mark is the first venture at saying the story of Jesus Christ, the Son of God, in *narrative* form. Mark effectively arranged series of events or sayings (we call them pericopes) in order to persuade. Mark has brought a remarkable achievement to a church that, as far as we know, had only the Pauline paradigm of death, burial, and resurrection, upon which Paul doesn't elaborate. Here comes Mark, a Christian writer, who tells the story in a narrative form, in such a way that, before the end, the readers know death, burial, and resurrection. It's there, but it's told in a story. Mark didn't diminish the importance of death/resurrection, but he presented it in narrative fashion. And there has been in recent time gravitation toward narrative with a great deal of delight. Mark gives us a narrative christology.

In preparation for this essay, I went through Mark to note how he preaches. It is Mark the *evangelist,* not the *book* of Mark, who unrolls the story of his narrative christology in an extremely effective way for preaching.

For instance, what I used to consider as nonliterary are Mark's connections, "And immediately. And immediately. And immediately." The first lesson I learned from Mark the preacher is the energy of his sermon. Mark's not laid back and cool as some preachers today try to be.

"This doesn't really make a lot of difference to me; if you'll sit still a few minutes, I'll be through." That's the kind of message I get from some preaching today.

Mark is on his tiptoes, high-energy; and Jesus is moving, moving, moving, and you're running to keep up with the story in high-energy motion. The first enemy of the church is the law of gravity. Didn't someone say that the major, primary task of Alexander when he tried to conquer the world (he got to the Hellespont) was that *he had to move*"? It sounds kind of silly, but it's true. The law of inertia will just destroy your church. A body at rest will tend to remain at rest unless an outside force moves it. We don't have to have a lot of theological jargon as to what's happening with the church. It's gravity and inertia. Preach like Mark preaches—something is going to happen. There's a stir, there's movement, there's tension in it.

Pay attention to the marvelous rhetorical and homiletical skill Mark displays in the unfolding of his narrative. Mark enrolls you as a participant. He makes you present for events that were otherwise private, and not of your knowledge.[3]

For example, Mark's sermon is full of people. There's a lot of population in his preaching. In many sermons that I hear, you don't see any faces. You hear ideas—sermons full of ideas and ideas and ideas. Listen to Mark preach. There are people all over, many of whom you know by name. I know the name of the man who carried the cross for Jesus. I know Bartimaeus's father's name. Realistic preaching has a lot of people in it. I hear some people preach who have great ideas, and they talk about "righteousness as we go forth today, seeking the stewardship of the kingdom as we try to achieve victories unto the present age in which we're living in this current and contemporary time." Doesn't mean a thing! Means absolutely nothing.

And some people say, "Well, the people liked my illustrations." The people liked your stories *because somebody was there*. There was a person in the illustration. Go through Mark and list the named and unnamed people in this short book. One reason Mark sustains interest is that Jesus meets so many people and does so many things. Read Mark 4. This woman had a hemorrhage, and she came up behind Jesus and said, "If I can just touch the hem of his—" And Jairus said, "My daughter is nearly dead. Won't you come?" And after a while they said, "Don't bother him anymore...She's dead." It's *people*.

So instead of preaching from Mark, let Mark be our instructor in preaching. Mark actually uses some attractive, strange words. He uses some Aramaic words, and it makes you feel like you're actually there. He says, "*Abba*." Do you remember what he said to Jairus's daughter? "*Talitha koum*." That's striking, *Talitha koum*.

I was in a church in San Antonio. The preacher was Hispanic, most of the congregation Hispanic, but he was preaching in English. In the middle of the sermon he used a Spanish sentence—and people stood up and applauded. I didn't know what all was going on, but it seemed to be a part of the original *healing* formula—*Talitha koum!* Look at the end of Mark 7. The man who couldn't speak and couldn't hear, and Jesus spit and touched the man's tongue, put his fingers in the man's ears, raised his voice to God and, with a *groan*—"*stenadzo*." With a groan, he says, "*Ephphatha!*" You're there! You're there—you're hearing it in the way it was said at the time! Why not?

Good preaching enrolls the listeners as participants. If there is a singular mark of what is called the New Homiletic, it is the increased responsibility of the listener to be participant in what is going on. I'm struck by Mark's use of the historic present tense. "And Jesus *enters*. And Jesus *goes* in to the Synagogue." He didn't say, "He *went* in." "Well, it's all past; why didn't he say, 'He went in?'" He *goes* in. Mark is like a journalist—you don't see a headline on a newspaper, *Man Fell From Twelfth Story Window;* It says *Man Falls From*...What does the journalist want you to experience? The actual event itself! If you make it past tense, you get the sense, "Well, I missed that fall, maybe others will fall." So, if sometime you break a leg skiing or get the mumps and have time laid up, go through Mark. Use your pencil, and underline the present tense in this story that's all past but told in the present. You are there!

Mark's language is so concrete and specific. Consider these paraphrases of Mark's narrative: "And the young man was wearing nothing but a linen cloth and they grabbed the cloth, and he ran away naked" (14:51–52). "He went over to the tree and found nothing but leaves—no figs" (11:13). "The crowd sat down on the green grass" (6:39). "Jesus was asleep on a cushion in the stern of the boat" (4:38). Notice the particularity of the language: "She put in two, small, copper coins" (12:42). "She broke open the jar and poured the ointment on his head" (14:3). "He threw himself on the ground"(14:35). It's remarkable language for a sermon. Why not?

Mark uses conversation. I miss this so much in preaching I hear. A text will be read, which is mostly conversation—"Jesus said, and the Pharisees said, Jesus said, and the Pharisees said,…" And you listen to the sermon on that passage, and there's no conversation. Conversation engages you; it gets you involved:

> And they entered Jericho, and there was in Jericho a blind man named Bartimaeus, his father—Timaeus. And when Jesus came by, he yelled out, "*Jesus, son of David*. Have mercy on me!" And the people said, "Hush!" But all the more he cried out "Jesus, son of David, have mercy on me," and Jesus said, "Call him over here." And they said, "He's calling for you. Go on over there." And he threw away his cloak and went over to Jesus; and Jesus said, "What do you want me to do for you?" And he said, "Rabboni…that I receive my sight." And Jesus said, "You have it." (Mk. 10:46–52 paraphrased)

That's a conversation! But you can preach a sermon on that text that is just sort of a bulletin on the board. Why not reconstruct the conversation? That's a very interesting thing, a very engaging *you are there* thing.

Little kid, on the sidewalk, near my house, riding his bicycle with a training wheel…It's a small bicycle. And as he went by, I said, "Hi."

And he said, "This is not a tricycle!"

I said, "I see it's not a tricycle. My, you're riding a bike."

And he said, "Yeah, and I go to school, too."

And I said, "You go to school?"
"Yeah, I go to school."
I said, "How old are you?"
And he said, "Six."
"And you're in school?"
"Yeah, I'm in school."
"You like school?"
"Yeah."
I said, "You learning anything?"
And he said, "Yeah, ask me, uh, ask me, uh, ask me…uh, what's eight and eight?"
I said, "All right, what's eight and eight?"
And he said, "Naw, uh, no, no, I mean, what's four and four?"
And I said, "What's four and four?"
And he said, "Aw,…I bet you don't know my name, do ya'?"
And I said, "No, I don't."
And he said, "Guess!"
And I said, "Tommy?"
"Naw."
"Timmy?"
"Naw."
"Sammy?"
"Naw."
"Johnny?"
"Naw."
"Clyde?"
"Naw." Then he said, "You give up?"
I said, "I give up."
He said, "My name is Kevin. Everybody at my school knows my name is Kevin." And he rode on—he had whipped me good.

Now you could change that into dull language by saying: "I was talking to this kid on the sidewalk and learned that he was in school and was six years old, and his name was Kevin," and such, and finish with, "Any questions?" "Yes, will this be on the test?" "Well…" Why not just reproduce the conversation—the conversation between Bartimaeus and Jesus? Conversations with all the characters is powerful.

Mark uses restraint in telling, which is a remarkable feat. I don't see how he does it really. How brief is the telling of many things! The actual account of the death of Jesus is very brief. Mark doesn't go on and on and on. I heard a horrible sermon on the death of Jesus on Good Friday when churches come together and every preacher in town has a part. The one who preached talked about the death of Jesus for thirty minutes. Much of the time was occupied by the preacher saying, "And his blood came down from his head and his hands and his feet...drip, drip, drip, drip, drip...," just stretching it out. The chaste, simple way Mark speaks is a lesson in homiletics.

Notice, too, the intensity of certain clusters of material in Mark. You experience that in Richard Ward's performance of Mark. You have, for instance, controversy stories clustered in 2:1—3:6, just one after another, five controversies. In chapter four, Mark collects several parables. Mark clusters miracles in 4:35—5:43. Intense and tight, Mark draws in the listener. This doesn't mean that Mark thought Jesus got up one morning and said, "Well, today's my controversy day." And the next day, "Today's parable day." Next, "miracle day." No, think of what you do when you cluster in rapid-fire fashion material that has cumulative effect—such as when you get to the end of those controversies: "And they took counsel with the Herodians how they could kill him" (3:6).Wow! Right there in the heart of the sermon!

Mark knows how to create anticipation by delaying a part of a story. *"And Jairus, the ruler of the synagogue asked, 'Can you come, my daughter's ill?'"* (5:22–23). And as they were making their way to his house, this woman came up behind. Mark delays the tale of Jairus with a long section about this woman with a hemorrhage whom Jesus heals. And then Jesus engages her in conversation and—oh, my goodness, the time is passing. Finally they say, "Leave the teacher alone, the girl is dead." At last Jesus makes his way to Jairus's home. You see, the story within the story gives everybody time to *feel* the tension, and *feel* the importance of what's about to happen.

At the trial of Jesus, they take Jesus to the house of Caiphas, the high priest. Simon Peter is in the courtyard when the camera goes back inside the house to Jesus and the high priest. Next, you are there with Simon Peter. Conscious literary art communicates.

And in the day when people's ears were not lazy, within the space really of less than two hours, they could hear Mark's entire story. He kept their attention through these extraordinary rhetorical devices.

At times Mark is following the principle of end stress, putting at the end what is most important. You know how that works; you save the best part to the very end. So much of the gospel narratives (narrative christology) are the crucifixion/resurrection of Jesus. It moves that way. The principle of end stress is here in Mark. For over half of the book, Jesus is in power, healing and exorcising. He turns and goes to Jerusalem. In Jerusalem there are no miracles. The only miracle in that area is the cursing of the fig tree. Now if I, in my stupidity, were working this into a sermon, I'd have the weak part first (Jesus being victimized, mistreated, suffering, dying), and have the whammy come next. Start in Jerusalem, and go to Galilee where the power was. Have everyone on their feet at the end. But Mark starts in Galilee with all the manifestations of power and ends on the cross, with a *word* about resurrection. Is that the way he wants to do it? Absolutely. Absolutely because the end displays the power above all powers, the miracle greater than anything he ever did in Galilee. It's remarkable.

Other writers do it; I don't mean to say that Mark is the only one. John talks about Jesus and the two others on the cross—they came to the first malefactor and broke his legs, they came to the second and broke his legs, then they came to Jesus; and he was already dead. Now where was Jesus? Was he on the end? First malefactor, second malefactor, and then Jesus? No! Jesus was in the middle. But how would it be if he said they came to the first malefactor and broke the legs, came to Jesus and he was already dead, and then went to the other one? No, no, no, no! The subject is Jesus!

So, the principle of end stress is that you tell the main point last. You know that already. Mark knows that. But what happens when we use biblical material as a mass of raw material? We think we have to fix the Bible with a lot of clever stuff about the time Uncle Fred fell out of the airplane, or about Aunt Myrtle's pink medicine. Or, "This'll get 'em. They'll love this—I have to find some more illustrations." Let Mark instruct us on how to handle all materials.

Formation and Information

The noises being made about the text now are that it's both informative and formative. It is information, and it is formation. Both are tasks of the church. We usually assign to the academy the task of handling the scripture as information. Deal with the information. Get people in here who know the material and can handle the information. The larger community, the church, is to use that for the formation of Christian character and community.

But there is an increasing recognition today that both of these are not only legitimate, but necessary uses of the text. People expect formation, not just information.

Sometimes graduate students wonder whether or not the professor believes anything, thinking of a white-jacketed, neutral person who deals with footnotes and references to something in Latin or Greek. What has all this got to do with preaching the gospel on Sunday morning? It has everything to do with it. If there isn't somebody responsible in the critical community for handling the text as information, then there's nothing for us to use in formation except our witty, clever, and imagined stuff.

What happens if the information dimension of our work is not carefully attended? We wind up with religion as generic spirituality, without content, a residue of reverence without belief. Or, as Alexander Campbell once said, it's "like trying to plant a tree on a cloud."

I think if it were not for those who deal in expertise with prayerful care over the text as *information*, the church would eventually sink into superstition and a bog of blessed assurance. Nothing there. So I appreciate those who taught me, even though I criticized them to their backs, not to their faces. I questioned their faith and their commitment, thinking they just come up out of that library basement for air, eat a little dried peanut butter sandwich, and go back down there. I thought, "Boy, what a horrible existence." But out of their effort comes another Greek Testament carefully prepared over twenty years by people who devote their lives and are no less ministers than those of us who are out thundering about—or piccoloing—in the pulpit somewhere.

That faith community, a critical community, deals with the text as information. The larger faith community has the power of formation of Christian community and Christian character. We believe that. I notice (maybe this is postmodern) a growing interest in this. Wayne Meeks, brilliant New Testament scholar, reminded us in a lecture recently, "Remember that the primary function of the New Testament is formation. Let's not get too carried away with the information." That was the scholar talking. And I notice more and more books are saying this. I recall an essay by Princeton's Clifton Black.[4] It's an exegesis of the Lord's Prayer: We are formed by that prayer. Pray that prayer every Sunday, and it makes a stamp upon you that will never leave. Read the New Testament every day; it will shape your life in a way that will never leave. Of course, you'll complain, "I can't remember any of it." Oh yes, yes, yes, you do. Inescapably, you do.

Conclusion

I don't know, really, what New Homiletic is. I've had a pleasant, rewarding, and satisfying career trying to figure it out. I hope you will continue to take advantage of volumes like this to let other people encourage you to find your voice. You can waste a lot of time imitating somebody else trying to be a bass drum when you're actually a trombone. God did not call you to give voice to a message without giving you the voice. You just have to find it.

3

This Is the Good News

The Challenge of Mark's Beginning

MORNA D. HOOKER

Introduction

Imagine, if you will, that you are gathered together, not in a spacious lecture hall in twenty-first–century America, but in a room in a house somewhere in the Roman Empire, toward the end of the first century C.E. You have met, as a group of Christians, to worship and to learn more about your faith. Normally, you would expect, at your meeting, to sing psalms, to pray, to hear readings from the scriptures—scriptures that we know today as the Old Testament—and to hear stories about what Jesus had done and said, possibly from someone who had met him. But today's gathering is a very special event, because someone—is it perhaps Mark himself?—has brought a copy of the very first written gospel—the gospel according to Mark—and is about to read it to us.

What an extraordinary impact his words have on us, as we hear them for the very first time! Mark's style is forceful and dramatic. He does not begin, as the later evangelists did, with a genealogy, or a literary preface, or a philosophical explanation. Mark begins with but a brief quotation from scripture, which serves to introduce John the Baptist, whose appearance, habits, and preaching are briefly described. "And immediately"—to borrow Mark's favorite phrase—after this account of John's preaching,

Jesus himself appears on the scene; and we learn more about who he is. From this point on, to the end of the story, the spotlight is almost continually on the figure of Jesus.

You will notice how the language I have used, almost inevitably, is the language of drama. Listening to Mark's gospel—and that, of course, is the way that the first Christians would have been introduced to it, since copies were rare and precious—was rather like being at a play: reading, with one dramatic scene followed immediately by another. Indeed, just as *we* are imagining ourselves back in that first-century house, sharing the experience of these early Christians, so *they* may well have been imagining themselves in one of the many amphitheatres in the ancient world. They had only to close their eyes to see, in their imaginations, the scenes being described by Mark unfold on the stage in front of them.

But what, you may well ask, had Christian worship to do with plays in a Roman or Greek amphitheatre? Surprisingly, perhaps, far more than we might expect, for if you visit the classical sites in the Mediterranean countries you will often see a temple situated near the amphitheatre. Nor is this simply because the public buildings were grouped conveniently together, for the plays staged in the theatres were often *sacred* sagas, relating the stories of the gods and goddesses worshiped in the temples. The people flocked to religious festivals. As part of their worship, they attended the plays and heard the stories about their gods. And now Christians, attending worship, were listening to a drama about what God had done through the life, death, and resurrection of his Son, Jesus Christ. Converted pagans in Mark's audience would have felt at home.

The Prologue

And why, you may be wondering, would those early Christians be imagining themselves in a theatre, rather than as part of the crowd in Galilee, listening to Jesus' teaching, or among the small group of disciples, following him, with trepidation, to Jerusalem? Well, maybe as the story progressed they did; that, after all, is the effect that any great drama has—to make us feel that we are present, taking part in the events enacted on the stage. We are drawn into the action, challenged by what we see and hear. Surely that is precisely what happens as Mark's story unfolds. But that is not, I suggest, how those first-century Christians would have felt while they heard the first thirteen verses of the gospel being read. For these thirteen verses are rather different from the rest of the story.

Whether by accident or by design, Mark's gospel is in many ways similar in its construction to many classical plays. One feature of these plays was the introductory "prologue," which provided the information necessary to understanding the play—the kind of information often provided today in a printed program. The prologue introduced the main characters and gave the audience some insights into the nature of the drama they were about to see performed on the stage. Sometimes a chorus recited this prologue and might well reappear from time to time in the course of the narrative to remind the audience of the significance of events. The men and women whose story the play presented did not share these insights—which is, of course, the reason why they so often made the wrong choices and did the wrong thing. Only the gods, it was believed, understood the full significance of what was happening at the time an event occurred. But now, *after* the event, the dramatist could share these insights with his audience.

The first thirteen verses of Mark's gospel provide us with that kind of information. We learn that the story is "gospel," i.e., "good news," is about someone called Jesus—who is the Messiah, or God's anointed—and is, in a very special sense, the Son of God. We learn, too, that what happens through him is the fulfillment of God's promises in the Old Testament. The story we are about to hear, then, is not one that we would expect to encounter in a Greek theater, for it belongs firmly within the Jewish world. Jewish listeners would have been familiar with these verses from the scriptures and would have been reassured that what they were about to hear concerned the continuing activity of the God whom they trusted and worshiped. Then Mark tells us that John the Baptist, clearly identified as a prophet—indeed, as the returning prophet Elijah—has announced the imminent coming of the Lord. John has prepared "the *way* of the Lord" and pointed forward to one who will baptize with the Holy Spirit. When we hear the divine voice at Jesus' own baptism and see the Holy Spirit descend on him, we realize that this is the one about whom John has been speaking. Finally, we are told that Satan has tested Jesus in the wilderness.

As Mark's story unfolds, we realize that none of the characters in the story, with the exception of Jesus himself, is aware of any of these things. The crowds flocked to hear John's message; but they did not know about whom he was speaking, understand the significance of the scripture, see the Spirit descend on Jesus, or hear the divine voice. Neither were they present in the wilderness when Satan tested Jesus. Mark privileges us, the audience, with information concealed from the participants in the story.

In many ways, then, these first thirteen verses stand apart from the rest of Mark's narrative. Here, as nowhere else (with the exception of the transfiguration in chapter 9) we are provided with clear, unambiguous information about who Jesus is: We see and hear what is concealed from the characters in the story. Here, and here alone, the evangelist (rather than Jesus or his opponents) quotes scripture and so provides the key to understanding the story. Here, and here alone, we have John pointing to Jesus (even though he does not name him) as the one who is so much greater than himself. Here alone we see the Holy Spirit descend on Jesus, and though the words from heaven will be repeated at the transfiguration, where three of the disciples as well as Jesus hear them, they are heard in 1:11 by Jesus alone. Finally, we have here the unusual reference to Jesus being tested by Satan in the presence of wild beasts, and being served by angels.

Mark shares his understanding of the story of Jesus with his readers—his hearers—from the very beginning. As preachers, we share his viewpoint. How then are we, as preachers, to handle these opening verses? Since they stand apart from the rest of the gospel, we should, I believe, treat them differently. In the rest of his narrative, Mark describes the words and actions of Jesus and the impact he had on other people. We are told of the amazement of the crowds, of the faltering attempts of his disciples to understand him, and of the growing hostility of the religious authorities. But in these first few verses, neither the crowds nor the disciples nor the religious authorities are privy to the information offered to us, so the focus is on Jesus alone. What the evangelist shares with us here are the insights, which enable us to read the subsequent story with the eyes of faith.

The temptation to read Mark's first thirteen verses in the light of the parallel accounts in Matthew and Luke is obvious. It is important that in expounding Mark we forget what we know as a result of studying the *other* gospels. It is always a mistake to read details from one gospel into another, and in preaching from Mark, we need to forget what Matthew and Luke tell us about John's teaching, for Mark concentrates on one aspect of John's preaching and ignores the rest of what he said. We need to forget, too, the fact that Matthew and John both believed that John recognized Jesus as the one whose coming he had proclaimed. In Mark's account, Jesus alone heard the divine voice and saw the Spirit descend on him. We should not suppose, however, that Mark has provided the material for us to recreate an account of Jesus' vocation to ministry. Mark was apparently uninterested in this question. He tells us only that Jesus was aware that he stood in a unique relationship to God, not *how* he came to believe this. Nor should we speculate about the nature of the temptations Jesus endured based on what Matthew and Luke tell us about them. Mark tells us only that he was tested by Satan. We must beware, then, of attempting to describe Jesus' "spiritual experience" on the basis of what Mark tells us.

These verses *do* tell us the way Mark wants us to interpret his story. When questions are raised, in the subsequent narrative, about who Jesus is and about what is taking place, we need only to think back to these introductory verses to comprehend their meaning.

In my book on *"Beginnings,"*[1] I attempted to analyze the information Mark provided in these first few verses. I should like now to try to do something rather different: Instead of concentrating on what makes these verses *distinctive*, I shall attempt to consider the *links* between what we are told here and the rest of the gospel. In other words, I intend to analyze some of the ways in which these verses help us to understand the rest of Mark's story. And since these links indicate the meaning of the narrative, they are of particular importance to preachers.

The Gospel about Jesus Christ

The opening words of the gospel—"The beginning of the good news of Jesus Christ" are an enigma. Are they intended as the title of the book—the equivalent of the liturgical, "Here beginneth the first lesson"—or are they merely the first few words of the opening sentence? And what *is* the beginning? Is it the promises of God in scripture that are the beginning of the good news? Is it the baptism carried out by John? Or is it the ministry, death, and resurrection of Jesus? In other words, is what we now call "Mark's gospel" merely the "beginning" of the good news—the beginning of an ongoing story that his followers still tell? That is an idea to which we must return when we look at Mark's ending.

Yet another ambiguity marks these opening words. Is Mark referring to the good news *about* Jesus Christ or to the good news announced *by* Jesus Christ? The Greek genitive can mean either. But since the whole of the prologue concentrates our attention on Jesus himself, it seems likely that Mark is thinking of the good news *about* Jesus Christ. If we turn on to verse 14, however, we find a very similar phrase used in a somewhat different sense. Here, at the very beginning of the "story proper," we discover the first of our links between the "prologue" and the rest of the book, for in verse 14 the word *euangelion*, meaning "gospel" or "good news," is used again. We are told that Jesus came into Galilee proclaiming the good news. To be sure, some scholars include verses 14 and 15 in the prologue,[2] and some translations—for example, the NRSV— print it as such. But if I am right in understanding the prologue as primarily providing us with the information we need to understand the rest of the story, then these verses must belong to the story proper, not to the prologue. But what is the good news Jesus proclaimed? Once again, we have a genitive, this time referring to God. It seems likely that we should translate the phrase here as "the good news *from* God" rather than "*about* God."

Does that mean that in verse 1 we should, after all, understand Mark to be writing about the good news announced *by* Jesus Christ? I suggest not. These two phrases provide us with a demonstration of what it means to see the events that Mark describes through his eyes. If you arrive at the theater late, and miss the opening scenes of Mark's story, your first impression will be of an itinerant preacher named Jesus, who travels through Galilee proclaiming a message of good news from God. You will be in the same position as the members of the crowd, who are amazed at what they see and hear, but totally incapable of explaining it. But if you listen to those first few verses, then you will see the scene in 1:14–15 through *Mark's* eyes—the eyes of faith. You will comprehend that though what Jesus proclaims is the imminent arrival of the kingdom of God, he himself is, in fact, the embodiment of that kingdom, for God is at work in and through him. When Jesus announces that the kingdom has "drawn near," we know that this is because it has drawn near in him. The message of Jesus—the good news proclaimed *by* him— has become the good news *about* him.

This good news, then, is about Jesus *Christ*, Jesus the Messiah. This clear declaration that Jesus is the expected Messiah will be reiterated only at the end of the story, when Jesus declares, "I am," in response to the high priest's question as to whether he is indeed the Messiah. But once again, there are links with other scenes in the story. At Caesarea Philippi, Peter will declare: "You are the Messiah," even though he clearly does not understand the signifi- cance of his own words. To us, the audience, what finally begins to dawn upon Peter at this point has been plain from the very beginning. We are not surprised to listen to Jesus' authoritative teaching, or to watch him bring healing to the sick, for Mark has assured us from the very beginning that he is God's anointed. But even *we* may find ourselves perplexed as the story unfolds, revealing his humiliation and crucifixion. Yet at this point in the story the links with 1:1 become clear: for Mark insists that Jesus is put to death, not *in spite of* the fact that he is Messiah, but precisely *because* he is the Messiah. He is proclaimed as King of Israel on the cross.

Scripture

Having established that we can expect to hear good news about Jesus the Messiah, Mark begins with a quotation from scripture. He is quoting, he tells us, the words of Isaiah the prophet. And as we all know, Mark gets the reference wrong! The second part of the quotation is, indeed, from Isaiah; Mark is indeed quoting Isaiah 40:3 when he tells us of

> [T]he voice of one crying out in the wilderness:
> "Prepare the way of the Lord,
> Make his paths straight."

The introductory words, however, are from Exodus and Malachi. A pedantic scribe corrected Mark, and changed "the prophet Isaiah" to "the prophets." In doing so, he may well have obscured something that Mark believed to be important.

Why did Mark attribute the words to Isaiah alone? Did he simply make a mistake? Did he perhaps not notice that some of the words came from elsewhere? Or was it, in a sense, a *deliberate* mistake? Was he perhaps concerned to draw our attention to the book of Isaiah, where so many of the promises about God's future salvation of his people are to be found? And why did he—unlike Matthew and Luke—use those words from Exodus and Malachi at this point in his narrative, rather than later on? We must return to that question in a moment, but first we must consider whether Isaiah was of particular importance to Mark.[3]

As we have noted already, this is the only Old Testament quotation in Mark's own comment on events. Others appear in the mouth of either Jesus or someone questioning him. Many of these are from Isaiah. Mark's specific mention of Isaiah in 1:2 suggests that quotations from Isaiah are of particular importance to him. His quotation of Isaiah 40:3 in his opening paragraph suggests that it is intended to help us understand the other quotations. But when we turn to them, they appear, at first sight, to be conveying a very different message.

The first of these is in one of the most difficult passages in the gospel: Mark 4:12. This time Isaiah is not specifically mentioned, but in words clearly reminiscent of Isaiah 6:9–10, Jesus is said to have told his disciples that he teaches the people in parables, "in order that they may look and look, yet perceive nothing; and that they may listen and listen, yet understand nothing. For otherwise they might turn and be forgiven" (author's translation).The problems with these words are obvious. Did Jesus really teach in parables in order that his hearers should not understand? The statement seems to clash with what Mark tells us elsewhere—e.g., in 4:33–34, where he comments that Jesus taught the people "the word…as they were able to hear it," and that he used parables to do so. It seems to clash, too, with the opening words of a book that speaks of "good news" and then quotes the promises of Isaiah 40:3. Mark 4:11–12 offers an explanation as to why so many of Jesus' fellow Jews failed to respond to his message. Seeing and hearing the good news are not enough: It needs to be perceived and understood. The salvation that Jesus offers must be grasped. Those who fail to respond are not ready for the coming of the Lord announced in Isaiah 40:3. The messenger promised there had come; he had prepared the way, by calling on the people to repent, and had promised forgiveness to those who did so. Mark 4:12 reminds us that God's purpose was indeed that men and women should turn to him and be forgiven.

We need to read Mark 4:11–12 in the light of that introductory quotation in 1:3. The good news Jesus proclaimed concerns salvation; but the way of the Lord is a way of righteousness, and the straight path demands sacrifice. Those who refuse to respond to God's offer of salvation will inevitably remain unforgiven. The Day of the Lord means salvation—but it also means judgment.

Mark's next quotation from Isaiah, in 7:6–7, seems equally negative. On this occasion, Jesus is said to be addressing the Pharisees and scribes, who are criticizing the actions of his disciples. This time, Isaiah is mentioned by name. Isaiah was speaking of them, Jesus says, when he declared:

> This people honors me with their lips,
>> but their hearts are far from me;
> in vain they worship me,
>> teaching human precepts as doctrines.[4]

Once again, Isaiah's words condemn those who are not ready for the coming of the Lord. And once again, they help to explain why so many of Jesus' contemporaries failed to respond to his message. This quotation, too, needs to be seen in the wider context of the message in 1:2–3. The Lord is here—offering salvation—but if men and women refuse to respond, judgment must follow.

A more positive quotation from Isaiah occurs in Mark 11:17, in the story we know as "the cleansing of the temple." Jesus quotes the words of Isaiah 56:7—"my house shall be called a house of prayer for all the nations." But though the words are positive, the context is negative, for Mark interprets Jesus' actions in the temple as a sign of coming destruction.[5] Just as the fig tree is destroyed because it is barren, so the temple will be destroyed, because the worship offered there is empty. But does that mean that Isaiah's words have proved false? Hardly! Mark's introductory quotation reassures us that God's promises are being fulfilled, in spite of human obstancy. And, indeed, we find hints in Mark's narrative about how this will be possible. The people may have prevented God's house from being a house of prayer, but God is about to raise a new temple. Jesus will be the "cornerstone" of a new building.[6] The promise in Isaiah will finally be fulfilled.

The next reference to Isaiah is not a quotation, but its origin is clear, nevertheless. Jesus' parable of the vineyard in Mark 12 picks up the image of Israel as God's vineyard in Isaiah 5. This parable introduces the second block of public teaching in Mark's gospel. The first came in chapter 4, introduced by the parable of the sower, which told of the promise of a bumper harvest, contrasted with possible failure. This final parable tells of another harvest—and another kind of failure. The vineyard has certainly produced a crop, but the tenants have failed to hand it over to the owner. Here, too, Isaiah appears to be used in a negative way—yet once again there is a note of promise. The vineyard tenants kill the owner's son and bring down terrible judgment on their own heads; but the vineyard itself is not destroyed, for it is given to others. And the rejected stone is made the cornerstone of the new building. Salvation and judgment go hand in hand.

Finally, in 13:24–25, we find a composite quotation that includes words from Isaiah 13:10 and 34:4, a quotation that appears to speak of the destruction of the universe. This is the language of apocalyptic, used to describe God's judgment and condemnation. Yet the picture is not entirely dark, for in 13:10 we are told that before this happens the good news will be proclaimed among the nations, and in 13:26–27 we are assured that the Son of Man will come and gather his elect. Even here, Mark affirms that God's promise for his people has not failed. Back in 1:2, he declared that the words of Isaiah were being fulfilled and that we must expect the coming of the Lord. His narrative has described that coming, and now we realize what we should have understood from the beginning: that it inevitably brings judgment as well as salvation.

John the Baptist

But why did Mark confuse us by including those words from Exodus and Malachi at the very beginning of his gospel rather than using them later on, as do Matthew and Luke?[7] Interestingly, the effect of starting with the words, "See, I am sending my messenger ahead of you, / who will prepare your way," is to put John firmly in his place. When John appears, in verse 4, we know already that he is only a voice, a messenger. We recognize that his sole function is to point forward to the one who follows him. John is Jesus' forerunner, and his dress and food authenticate him as the expected prophet. In contrast to Matthew and Luke, who provide fuller reports of his teaching, John's proclamation in Mark consists of three brief statements, all of which concentrate our attention on the one who is so much greater than John himself.

Once again we see links between this section of the prologue and the rest of the narrative. The first comes in verse 14, for the opening words of the narrative proper are, "After the handing-over of John…" (author's translation). Mark uses the verb *paradidōmi*, a word he normally uses with reference to Jesus. Its meaning is ambiguous: it can mean both "to hand over" and "to betray." The Son of Man, we are told, is to be handed over, or betrayed. So when, having been informed that John is Jesus' forerunner, we find the narrative beginning with the words, "After the handing-over of John…," the implication is plain; if the prophet who prepares the way has been handed over, what will happen to the one who follows him?

In case we fail to comprehend the significance of John's fate for Jesus himself, Mark reminds us about it several times. In 6:7–29 we have a remarkable section in which Mark describes the death of John—remarkable because it is the only scene in the gospel when the focus is not on Jesus himself. Yet it is clear that the story is told precisely because of its relevance to Jesus. In its introduction, Herod wonders about who Jesus is: Is he John the Baptist raised from the dead? Or is he, as some suggest, a prophet, or the returning Elijah? We, of course, already know the answer to these questions, for we know that John was sent to prepare the way of the Lord. And now

Herod has been outwitted by those who desired John's death, much
as Pilate will be outwitted later in the story by those who wish to
destroy Jesus. John has been put to death, and his disciples have
taken his body and laid it in a tomb. What, then, will happen to
Jesus?

Jesus himself supplies the answer following the transfiguration.
Surely, the disciples ask, "Must Elijah come first, to prepare the
way?" Smug in the knowledge that we have gained through
watching the prologue, we understand when Jesus replies, "Elijah
has [already] come." But there is more. "Look," he adds, "what
they have done to him!"—then he asks, "So what will they do to
the Son of Man?" (author's translation).

The relationship between John and Jesus is discussed again in
Mark 11. Here the religious leaders challenge Jesus' authority. He
throws the question back, asking *them* about John's authority. Jesus
may seem to be trying to evade their question; but to us, who are
familiar with Mark 1:1–13, his meaning is clear. John had prepared
the way for Jesus. Was John's authority from God, or was he an
impostor? The people had recognized John as a prophet, but if
John's authority was indeed from God, then Jesus' authority must
come from God also.

John was a voice, crying in the wilderness, "Prepare the way
of the Lord." Men and women flocked to hear him and to be
baptized—just as later they flocked to hear Jesus. But had they
truly repented? Clearly, many had not. It is hardly surprising, then,
if they then rejected the one whose coming John had announced.

John's Baptism

John's message compares his own role with that of his successor. His final comparison is the most intriguing: "I have baptized
you with water," he says; "he will baptize you with the Holy Spirit."
Commentators tend to emphasize the contrast: on the one hand,
we have baptism with water; on the other, baptism with the Holy
Spirit. In the light of our knowledge of Acts 2, we all think forward
to what happens after the death and resurrection of Jesus, when
the Holy Spirit is poured out on the believing community. But Mark
concludes his story well before that event. Mark did not write Acts.
If we should beware of interpreting his gospel in the light of Luke's,
we should certainly beware of interpreting it in the light of Acts. It
may be, of course, that Mark believed that John was pointing
forward here to an experience that came later. This seems to me

unlikely, however, since everything else in John's message points to the imminent arrival of his successor, and so concentrates our attention on what Jesus is going to do *during his ministry*. Should we not expect this "baptism with the Holy Spirit" to take place when Jesus appears on the scene?

Our mistake, I think, is to emphasize the *contrast* between John and Jesus. Mark, however, as we have just seen, stresses the *continuity* between them. True, Jesus is much greater than John; but John prepares the way for Jesus, both in his proclamation and in his suffering and death. He prepares the way for him, also, we may add, in his *baptism*. John came, Mark tells us, *proclaiming* baptism; his baptism, like his message, announced what was about to happen. John's baptism, I suggest, should be understood as a prophetic sign, similar to those performed by prophets such as Jeremiah and Ezekiel.[8] The prophetic sign—like the prophetic word—proclaims the message that the prophet has received from the Lord. What, then, would we expect a baptism with water to symbolize? In the Old Testament and intertestamental literature, water is a symbol of cleansing.[9] John himself is said to have spoken of his baptism as pointing toward the forgiveness of sins. Being submerged under the water can also have a negative significance; when the waters overwhelm one, then they are a symbol of judgment.[10] But water is also a symbol of renewal and of new life.[11] All these ideas are appropriate to the message of the voice, which called on his fellow Israelites to prepare for the coming of the Lord.

What is the baptism with Spirit to which John's baptism points, the baptism that the Lord himself will bring? This, too, brings judgment and forgiveness, through purging. Isaiah speaks of the Lord "washing away the filth of the daughters of Zion, and cleansing the bloodstains of Jerusalem by a spirit of judgement and a spirit of burning."[12] (author's translation). God's spirit also brings renewal. In Isaiah 44, for example, God promises to bring renewal to his people by pouring out his Spirit upon them. Since the images of "water" and of "Spirit" are used in similar ways, it is hardly surprising to find that they can be used side by side, as they are here: "I will pour water on the thirsty land, / and streams on the dry ground; / I will pour my spirit upon your descendants, / and my blessing on your offspring" (Isa. 44:3–4). Similarly, Ezekiel 36:25–27 states: "I will sprinkle clean water upon you, and you shall be clean… I will put my spirit within you." And if we turn to the Qumran literature, we find the promise that a member of the community "shall be cleansed from all his sins by the spirit of holiness." The following statement promises his flesh is to be "sprinkled with purifying water and sanctified by cleansing water" (1 QS 3:6–9).

If I am right in understanding John's baptism as a prophetic sign, then it points to the baptism with Spirit Jesus brought. Water is a *symbol* of cleansing, of judgment, of life; but the Spirit *affects* these things, for to speak of the Spirit is to speak of God at work. So, is John pointing forward to a pouring out of the Spirit on Jesus' disciples after his death and resurrection? Surely not! He appears to be pointing to what will happen when the Lord arrives on the scene. Moreover, this seems to be the way in which Mark has understood his words, for he goes on to assure us that Jesus is indeed the one on whom God's spirit has descended and in whom the Spirit is at work.[13]

If Jesus baptizes men and women with the Holy Spirit, we expect to see him bringing them purging, forgiveness, judgment, healing, new life. John's water baptism is a symbol of these things—a proclamation of what is to come—but Jesus brings the reality by baptizing men and women with the Holy Spirit. If we read the rest of Mark's gospel in this light, we see that this is precisely what he does. If we accept the usual interpretation of John's words in 1:8, the promise that Jesus will baptize with the Holy Spirit is still unfulfilled when we reach the end of the book. I am suggesting that this promise is fulfilled the moment Jesus comes into Galilee in 1:14 and proclaims the kingdom of God.[14] As though to confirm this, we find in Mark 3:28–30 the link that points us back to the prologue. Immediately before, in verse 22, the religious leaders have accused Jesus of working through the power of Satan, or "Beelzebul," as he is termed here. Satan has already appeared in the prologue, for the first thing the Spirit did after descending on Jesus was to drive him into the wilderness to do battle with Satan. Those of us who watched those early scenes will be aware of the irony of the accusation now brought against Jesus. In reply, Jesus is said to have underlined that what he was doing was the work of the Holy Spirit. Already he has brought forgiveness (2:1–12) and new life to the sick (1:40–44; 3:1–6, 9–10) and has purged those possessed by unclean spirits (1:21–27; 3:11). Now he brings judgment to those who refuse to recognize that the Holy Spirit is at work in him and who ascribe his deeds to Satan. If John by his action baptized the people with water, then Jesus is surely baptizing them with Holy Spirit.

Son of God

At his baptism, Jesus is not only identified as the one in whom God's spirit is at work, but is declared by the divine voice to be God's beloved Son, with whom he is well pleased. This declaration, like everything else in these opening verses, is, of course, unusual, though something very similar occurs in chapter 9. But once again, links with other passages in the gospel appear. In 12:1–9, Jesus tells the parable about the vineyard, reminding us of Isaiah's image of Israel as "the vineyard of God." In the parable, the owner has a beloved son. Those of us who overheard the divine voice in 1:11 inevitably put two and two together. In 14:62, the high priest is said to have asked Jesus directly whether he is "the Son of the Blessed One." Jesus replies, "I am." Most remarkable of all are his executioner's words at the moment Jesus dies: 'Truly this man was God's Son!" (15:39). At Caesarea Philippi, Peter grasped a part of the truth when he confessed Jesus to be God's Messiah, though he then demonstrated that he had no understanding of what that might mean. Now, at the end of the story, a despised Gentile— more amazing still, a member of the occupying army—becomes the first human being to acknowledge that Jesus is God's Son.

We have noted already the link between Mark's account of the temptation and the confrontation in 3:21–30. There is, of course, another link. Peter, immediately after acknowledging Jesus to be God's Messiah, insists that he cannot suffer. Jesus' words to him, "Get behind me, Satan," suggest that Jesus is once again being tested. The way he must follow is the way of obedience, and that will mean suffering. We may have yet another link between the account of the temptation and the rest of the story. Mark's mysterious reference to Jesus being accompanied by wild beasts in the wilderness and his comment that the angels waited on him remind us of what Psalm 8 has to say about the Son of man. Many modern translations have completely obscured the reference in the interests of political correctness. The Hebrew of Psalm 8:4 reads:

What is man that you are mindful of him,
And the Son of man, that you care for him?

The psalm then goes on:

You have made him a little lower than God,[15]
And crowned him with glory and honor;
You have given him dominion over the works of your hands;

You have put all things under his feet—
All sheep and oxen,
And also the beasts of the field.

God's original purpose for men and women is restored in Jesus, who is obedient to God's will and who resists Satan's temptation. In him, Adam's sin is reversed. The wild beasts acknowledge him as their master, and the angels serve him. No wonder, then, that in the rest of Mark's gospel, Jesus is said to have referred to himself as "the Son of Man"! Reading those references in the light of Psalm 8 may well help us to understand the claims to authority that Mark believes Jesus to be making.[16] The one who is well pleasing to God and who is obedient to him fulfills God's original purpose for Adam.

Conclusion

For the preacher, Mark's introduction provides a rich resource in itself. But it does more than this, for it offers illumination and inspiration to help us in our exposition of the whole gospel. Mark invites us to read the rest of the book in the light of the insights that he shares with us in these opening paragraphs. If we do so, we discover that this "prologue" points us to a deeper understanding of his message and that through it he challenges us to share his belief in the good news about Jesus Christ.

4

Believe and Follow

The Challenge of Mark's Ending

MORNA D. HOOKER

Introduction

Every time I fly into Heathrow, I wonder how many times the plane will circle around London before we finally touch down. Heathrow is one of the busiest international airports in the world. If a plane misses its "slot," it is put into the "stacks" and forced to circle round and round until the air controllers finally give the pilot permission to land. Interesting though it may be to see the bridges over the Thames and the houses of Parliament from the air, by the time I pass over them for the fifth or sixth time, I have had enough. The plane's circular route reminds me of an old gramophone record that has somehow got stuck in a groove—or perhaps of a preacher who does not know how to bring his sermon to a close. What a contrast, then, to read the ending of Mark's gospel, which appears to run out of fuel and dump us suddenly on the ground in the middle of nowhere.

"And the women fled from the tomb, overcome by fear and trembling; and they said nothing to anyone, for they were afraid" (16:8, author's translation). This, surely, is not the kind of ending you would expect from a preacher; not the way you would expect a book to end—least of all, a book that claims to be "good news." "But what," we demand, "happened next?" Which, of course, is precisely what Mark *wants* us to ask—and to answer for ourselves.

45

His final words invite us to continue the story in our own lives. Like all good evangelists, he concludes with a challenge.

In my little book on "*Endings*,"[1] I noted the fact that many of our Old Testament books conclude in an "open-ended" way. It is as though the last words in each book ran "to be continued in our next." The most obvious example is the book of Jonah, which ends with God asking a question: "And should I not be concerned about Nineveh, that great city, in which there are more than one hundred twenty thousand persons who do not know their right hand from their left, and also many animals?" (4:11). Although the question is posed to Jonah, it is clear that it is also being put to us, who listen to the story. *We* are being challenged by Jonah's story to understand more of God's compassion for all people. And so it is with Mark's ending. "Go," the women are told, "tell his disciples that Jesus is going before them to Galilee; they will see him" (16:7, author's translation). But are *we* not his disciples? Does that mean that if *we* go to Galilee, *we*, too, will see him there? If so, what does "going to Galilee" mean for us?

Mark appears to leave us stranded, his closing scene an empty tomb and a group of women, scared out of their wits. And after that, it would seem, nothing but silence. But this stark conclusion forces us to think and to act. Mark is apparently doing what some modern dramatists do—offering us, his audience, a choice regarding the final scene. He invites us to decide what comes next. Will we simply put the book down with a sense of disappointment, and say, "Well, that is the end of the story as far as I am concerned"? Or will we ask, "Where do I go from here?" Will we hear Mark's challenge and respond? If we do, then Mark's story will indeed be "the *beginning* of the good news" (1:1).

Like the prologue, the ending of Mark's gospel in many ways stands apart. One obvious difference from the rest of the book is that the central character in Mark's story does not appear, even though he is certainly the key figure in the narrative. For another, the supporting roles are played by the women, rather than the disciples. But if this final section stands apart from the rest of the book, what about possible links with the rest of the narrative? There are fewer of these than there were in the prologue, and fewer than there are in the endings of the other gospels, but links there are, nevertheless. Let us explore them.

Death and Resurrection

The first link is provided by the three women who come to the tomb to anoint Jesus' body and are told that he is not there. Have they perhaps come to the wrong tomb? That cannot be the case, however, because Mark has already named these women at the end of chapter 15, where he explains that they were present at Jesus' death (15:40–41) and two of them had watched his burial (15:47). Because they had been witnesses of his death and burial, they are able now to identify the tomb where he had been laid. At the beginning of the gospel, John the Baptist announced the coming of the Lord, an announcement followed immediately by Jesus' arrival from Nazareth (1:9). Even though John did not recognize Jesus, the way in which Mark juxtaposes the material means that he is able to use John to identify Jesus as the coming One. Now, at the end of the story, the women come seeking "Jesus of Nazareth, who was crucified" (16:6), and so discover and identify the empty tomb. Like John, the women are faithful servants of God and are used by him, even though they themselves have not yet seen the risen Lord and do not yet believe.

The women point us back to Jesus' death and burial. They remind us that the stories of Jesus' death and resurrection belong together. It is obvious, then, that we cannot watch Mark's final scene as though it were detached from the rest of the story. Jesus' death and resurrection are linked.

Since death and resurrection are so closely linked together, we clearly need to go back and read the passion narrative once more. But where does that begin? Mark's gospel has sometimes been described as "a passion narrative with a long introduction." The story of the passion dominates the book. Warnings of what lies ahead occur repeatedly throughout its second half. We commonly describe these warnings as "passion predictions," but in the light of Mark's ending, it becomes plain that this is somewhat misleading. All these predictions refer not only to Jesus' coming death, but also to his *resurrection:* "The Son of Man will be killed," we are told, "and three days later he will rise again."[2] *Suffering and vindication belong together*. When Jesus speaks of suffering, it is in the context of glory. When he speaks of glory, it is in the context of suffering.[3] Mark's story is not simply the story of Christ's passion, but the story of his vindication. Conversely, what Jesus promises his disciples is not just reward, but suffering![4] The two themes are inextricably bound together.

In our preaching, we sometimes make the mistake of concentrating on *either* the death of Jesus *or* the resurrection. It is natural enough, of course, that we should concentrate on his death on Good Friday and on his resurrection on Easter Sunday. But when we ignore one or other of these vital elements, we distort the significance of the other. The development of Christian doctrine has tended to link Christ's death, in particular, with the forgiveness of sin; but we misinterpret the significance of Jesus' death if we detach it from resurrection. His resurrection marks his vindication and demonstrates his acquittal. Only in the light of the resurrection can we understand the meaning of Jesus' death. The church celebrates the resurrection as the great victory; and so it is; yet all our evangelists imply that Christ's death itself was a victory! In Mark, we have seen how Jesus withstood the testing of Satan in the wilderness (1:12–13), and that Satan later tempted him again, by urging him to turn away from the cross (8:33). In Gethsemane, Jesus resisted temptation once again and accepted the cup of suffering (14:32–40). Is there not a sense in which Jesus is already vindicated at his death, when the temple curtain is torn in two and his executioner confesses him to be the "Son of God"? In the Fourth Gospel, the note of victory is even clearer, for Jesus dies with the triumphant words, "It is finished!" on his lips.

When Christians concentrate only on the suffering and death of Jesus, they tend to bewail their own sinfulness and to lose sight of the victory over sin that his resurrection brings. When they concentrate only on the resurrection, they tend to forget Jesus' command to his disciples to take up the cross and to follow him. Like the Corinthians, they rejoice in the new life, which Christ brings, and forget that they must first die to the old.[5] They think that discipleship entitles them to a reward, and they forget its cost.

Mark clearly believes that Jesus' words should have prepared the disciples for his betrayal and death. Whether or not Jesus did speak of these events as clearly as Mark suggests is, of course, a matter of debate; but as the evangelist looked back over what had happened, the implication of Jesus' teaching seemed plain. In Mark's view, the disciples should have been expecting Jesus' death; but that means that they should have been prepared also for his resurrection. It is hardly surprising, then, that the message entrusted to the women by the young man clothed in white at the empty tomb points back to what Jesus had told his disciples in 14:27–28. If Jesus' words about betrayal, suffering, and death have already been fulfilled, should they not now be expecting his words about resurrection and vindication to be fulfilled also?

The young man instructs the women to: 'Go, tell his disciples and Peter that he is going ahead of you to Galilee; there you will see him, just as he told you" (16:7). In Gethsemane, Jesus had told the disciples that the words of Zechariah 13:7 about the shepherd being struck and the sheep scattered were about to be fulfilled, but had promised them that when he was raised up again, he would lead them into Galilee. And Peter promptly protested, saying that he would never desert Jesus, a rash promise that evokes Jesus' prediction that he would betray him before cock-crow. That prediction, too, has been fulfilled. That being so, we can be confident that Jesus has indeed gone ahead into Galilee.

The young man's reference to Peter reminds us of Peter's shameful failure. But now, remarkably, Peter has been forgiven—remarkably, because if we think back to 8:38, we remember that Jesus warned his disciples that those who were ashamed of him would find that the Son of Man would be ashamed of them when he came in glory. That day has not yet arrived, however, and Peter still has a chance to begin again.

The disciples are instructed to go to Galilee. What does this "going to Galilee" involve? Is it just a convenient rendezvous, or is there some special reason for meeting there? Jesus came into Galilee in 1:14. There, in verse 16, he called his first disciples. Jesus is asking the disciples, who have failed him so miserably, to follow him back into Galilee. Does this mean that Jesus is telling them he is still prepared to have them (even Peter!) as his disciples and that this summons to Galilee is an invitation to begin the process of learning what discipleship means all over again?

"Go to Galilee." For the disciples, that means responding to the call of Jesus once more, and beginning again. Like college students who have failed an examination, they receive a chance to retake the course. And we, too, are being urged to look back, not just to the passion narrative, but also to the beginning of the gospel. We must certainly turn back to 1:14, since it was there that we heard how Jesus came into Galilee and summoned the first disciples. We need to reread the story in the light of what we now know. This time, we will surely see meaning in it that we did not grasp the first time, for the epilogue, like the prologue, enables us to understand the narrative in-between the beginning and the end. If we are to appreciate the relevance of what we discover in this final scene to what preceded it, we must reread the story all over again.

The Truth Revealed

We have already discovered we cannot understand what took place in Galilee unless we first read 1:1–13. This means we must surely go back to the very beginning and reread the gospel again from verse 1. What did we learn when we read these first thirteen verses for the first time? We found that they are packed with theological information about Jesus. We learned that his coming fulfils the promises made through Isaiah, that he is the one prophesied by John, that he is Messiah and Son of God and has resisted the temptation of Satan.

As we read Mark's story for a second or a third time, we shall read it with a deeper understanding of what we learned in those introductory verses, for the rest of the gospel has given us greater insight into what "messiahship" and "Sonship" mean. In pointing us back to Galilee, Mark is inviting us to read his story in the light of this fuller understanding of who Jesus is. We first read through Mark's gospel in the light of the first thirteen verses. We saw how what *we* already knew about Jesus was gradually revealed to others during the course of the narrative. In particular, we realized that the truth about who Jesus is was closely connected with his death and resurrection. We discovered, indeed, something that we had not understood from those introductory verses. Jesus' obedience to God and resistance to temptation would mean that he would be put to death, and that he would be put to death, not *in spite of* the fact that he was Messiah, but precisely *because* he was the Messiah. On the cross he is proclaimed as King of Israel. In his death he is revealed as Son of God. As we read his story again, it will be in the light of what we now know about his death and resurrection. Our second reading of Mark's gospel will be even richer than the first.

As early as Caesarea Philippi, we have Jesus' first warning about what lies ahead. The significance of Caesarea Philippi for Mark's story is that here, for the first time, part of the truth about Jesus is expressed by human lips. In the early chapters of the book, Mark tells us that men and women whom he describes as possessed by unclean spirits have apparently recognized Jesus; but their words seem to have fallen on deaf ears. Men and women have asked questions about Jesus, and the answers to their questions have seemed patently obvious to us, who have known the truth about him from the very beginning of the narrative. But the characters in the story are still stumbling after the truth.

Even at Caesarea Philippi, Peter is still stumbling. Throughout the rest of the story, he continues to stumble, as do the rest of the disciples. What causes them to stumble is the scandal of the cross. The disciples are unable to grasp that messiahship means suffering, that greatness comes through service, and that glory comes through death. The question of Jesus' identity is inextricably bound up with the forthcoming events in Jerusalem.

Caesarea Philippi marks a turning point in Mark's narrative because here, at last, one of Jesus' disciples articulates part of the truth about Jesus. Yet Peter does not really understand what he is saying, any more than he understands what he is saying in the next scene, the transfiguration, where he blurts out a request to build shelters for Jesus, Moses, and Elijah.[6] Peter will remain without understanding until he obeys that final command in 16:7. For Jesus, messiahship means suffering and death; but since he trusts in God, it also means vindication. Only when men and women understand this will they understand who he is. The failure of the disciples to comprehend the nature of Jesus' calling is demonstrated throughout the journey to Jerusalem: because they are blind to the truth, they address him as "rabbi" and quarrel about precedence. When we turn again to 16:7, we find that even the women are still uncomprehending: they are looking for "Jesus of Nazareth," we are told—or rather for his body. They have still not understood who he really is.

So how *should* they be thinking of him? As we come closer to the passion narrative itself, we see further glimpses of the truth. On the way between Jericho and Jerusalem, a blind man, with more insight than those who can see, acknowledges Jesus as "Son of David." When he is healed, he follows Jesus "on the way"—the way leading to Jerusalem, and so to suffering, death, and resurrection. That little phrase reminds us of what being "Son of David" involves. Then follows the story of Jesus' triumphant entry into Jerusalem. At this point, we notice a remarkable change in Jesus' behavior, for his actions now appear to be deliberate claims to authority. First, he rides into Jerusalem on the back of a donkey. We so often misunderstand this scene, because we assume that the donkey signifies humility, but Zechariah 9:9 speaks of a king who comes in peace and who is gentle, rather than humble. Pilgrims to the festivals in Jerusalem did not ride into the city—not even on donkeys—they walked! Yet Jesus, having walked all the way to Jerusalem from Galilee, deliberately rides. The scene is reminiscent of the scene in 1 Kings in which Solomon rides on the back of David's mule into Jerusalem and is proclaimed king.[7] Jesus enters Jerusalem, the place where he must suffer, as king. In the temple, he acts with extraordinary authority and teaches in a way that inevitably focuses our attention on him.[8] Then, instead of teaching his disciples in private, he teaches openly, in the temple; he challenges the people to respond.

In chapter 13, Jesus is reported as teaching his disciples about the future; here we find clear references to himself as Messiah, Son of Man, and Son of God.[9] Whatever we believe about the origin of this material in chapter 13, we can safely say that it makes far more sense to us than it could have made to the disciples. In the temple, Jesus had summed up the commandments by stressing the demand to love God and love one's neighbor (Mk.12:28–34). Now he utters a warning of judgment on those who have failed to do either.

I am intrigued by the correspondence between the two incidents that introduce and follow chapter 13. They stand like "bookends" to Jesus' words there, reminding us that some *have* responded. These two stories provide another link with 16:1–8, since—unusually—the central character in each of them is a woman. And like the women at the tomb, these women are portrayed as faithful; Jesus commends both of them. In the first incident, a poor widow throws everything she has into the treasury. She is contrasted with the religious teachers, the "scribes," who make a great show of religion, but who exploit the poor (12:38–44). She shows true devotion to God. In the second, a woman breaks a precious alabaster vase and pours its contents over Jesus' head. This woman is contrasted with bystanders who declare that the huge sum of money it was worth—at least three hundred denarii—should have been spent on the poor; she is contrasted, too, with Judas, who now arranges to betray Jesus for a paltry thirty denarii (14:3–11). She shows true devotion to Jesus.

With this second story, Mark's passion narrative really has finally begun. We have another link with the epilogue, for the woman's action is interpreted by Jesus as a preparation for his burial. Like John's baptism, it announces something else. But her action surely signifies more than burial. The truth about Jesus is becoming plainer. The woman does not pour the perfume over Jesus' feet, as might have been expected, but over his head. Solomon rode on his father's mule into Jerusalem and was anointed king by Zadok the priest; Jesus rides into Jerusalem on a borrowed donkey and is anointed—by a woman! The parallel is so absurd that we may well miss it—but it is there. Unaware of the significance of her action, this woman makes Jesus' identity plain to us. Jesus commends her, declaring that she will be remembered, wherever the gospel is proclaimed, for what she has done. Of course she will! For what her action symbolizes—his messiahship and his coming burial, linking his death and resurrection—this *is* the gospel! But the true irony of Mark's account is that the woman who is remembered has no name: we remember her, not for who

she was, but for what she did. Her love for Jesus really *is* unselfish, *good*
for like the widow in the temple, she is happy to give everything.

With Jesus' arrest, however, the truth about his identity is
brought out into the open. When Jesus is brought before the priests
and elders, the high priest asks whether he is the Messiah, the Son
of the Blessed. Without realizing it, he has spoken the truth, and
Jesus replies, "I am." When Pilate asks Jesus whether he is the King
of the Jews, he answers, "You say so." Jesus throws the responsibility of acknowledging who he is onto others—onto us: It is up to *us*
to decide who he is. Hearing the story for the first time, we might
well think, as do most of the characters, that what is happening is
a farce. Pilate continually refers to Jesus as "the King of the Jews,"
but he does not believe it. When Jesus is eventually condemned to
be crucified, the soldiers mock him as "King." He is dressed in
purple and given a crown of thorns. The inscription on the cross
reads "the King of the Jews." Passersby mock him as "Messiah"
and "King." No one believes he *is* King. But the final affirmation is
different, and it is astonishing, for his executioner, seeing him *die*,
acknowledges him as "Son of God."

Then Jesus is taken down from the cross and hastily buried.
Very early on the first day of the week, some women come to anoint
his body. And so we return to that final scene.

An Absurd Ending!

Imagine, if you will, that you are back in that theater, watching
the drama unfold for the first time. Imagine, if you can, that you
have not heard the story before and do not know how it will end.
Indeed, you suppose that with the death of Jesus, the story *has*
ended: that the burial of Jesus' corpse is the final scene in the
tragedy. A poor, deluded wandering preacher has come up against
the authorities and paid the price with his life. What you expect
now is merely a postscript, which will perhaps draw out the moral
of the tale or mourn the loss of such a great man. Instead, Mark
offers you an extraordinary scene at the tomb, which makes you
go back and reread the story, compelling you to see it in a new
light.

There is no escaping the fact that Mark's final scene *is* an extraordinary one. Yet in many ways it is typical of Mark. Commentators
have been arguing for centuries about the way in which he tells
his story—his clumsy grammar, repetitive style, strange
juxtapositions of material. Do these features show he was not a

particularly skilled writer? Had his education perhaps been somewhat basic? Or did he just not have the ability to turn out the kind of sophisticated piece of writing that Luke was able to write? If the ending strikes us as unpolished, so does the rest of the book.

Mark would certainly never have won the Nobel Prize for literature, and yet his writing is extraordinarily effective. His use of words and simple phrases, apparently so unsophisticated, nevertheless has extraordinary force.

And so it is in this final scene. Take its opening lines about the women setting out to the tomb early in the morning with their spices. Why? To anoint Jesus, Mark tells us. What an absurd statement! Suppose that you are reading this account in an essay presented by a college student; already you will have put a large red cross in the margin! The mission is impossible. The anointing should have been done *before* burial, you explain, not on the third day. By the third day, it is too late: in the Palestinian climate, the body must surely already be decomposing; to perform the task now is impossible.

But Mark knows, as the women knew, that it is too late. Why, then, do they set out on this absurd mission? Perhaps they had merely gone to mourn by the tomb, not to anoint the body. By explaining their purpose in this way, however, Mark points us back, as we have seen, to that other anointing, by the woman at Bethany. In fact *these* women have no need to anoint Jesus for burial. The task has already been done. They do not know this—but Mark knows it, and *we* know it. We know something else the women do not. Their task is impossible for another, even more important, reason. They cannot anoint Jesus' body because he has already been raised from the dead. They are too late because it is the third day.

Mark's final story begins, then, with an apparent absurdity, designed to make us aware of what is really going on, behind the scenes. And he follows it immediately by another. The women, on the way to the tomb, begin to ask one another, "Who is going to move the stone for us, so that we can enter?" Surely, if the stone was so large (as Mark insists that it was, v. 4), they would have had the common sense to take a strong man with them to move it for them. Or perhaps they would have needed several strong men, since three women apparently could not expect to move it.

It is possible to explain this absurd question by suggesting that Mark did not have a high opinion of the women's intelligence. I doubt, however, if that is why he tells us what they were discussing, for the question focuses our attention on two things. First, we realize they have not brought a strong man with them to move the stone not because they did not think of it before they set out, but because the men in their party are all in hiding. Disciples who fled from the garden and kept out of sight during the trials, the crucifixion, and the burial, will not wish to risk being seen at the tomb. The only one who had dared to show his face had been Peter, and after his experiences in the high priest's house, he is going to keep well out of sight. Only the women have the courage to be recognized as Jesus' friends. Who, then, can help them?

Second—and more important—the women's question draws our attention to the huge size of the stone. So Mark prepares us for their astonishment when they arrive at the tomb and discover that it has been rolled back. In this simple way Mark contrasts human failure—the fear of the disciples—with divine power. This power is such that the strong men are not, after all, required. The women's question is a clever dramatic device, ensuring that we realize that God himself has been at work.

At this point, we might expect the women to hesitate, but they do not. They boldly enter the tomb, where a young man in white confronts them. He assures them that Jesus has been raised and entrusts them with a message for the disciples. The disciples had failed to accompany the women, but they are not forgotten. Central characters in the story from the beginning, they still have an important role to play. In spite of their total failure, they are still being called to follow Jesus.

Mark's story began with a young man, John, dressed in garments identifying him as a prophet, standing by the River Jordan. He announced the one who was coming after him. He was, as it were, pointing off-stage, and saying, "He is coming!" What was the proper response? Why, to follow the one who was coming! When Jesus came into Galilee, the disciples followed. Now Mark's story ends with another young man, this time dressed in white—a color that presumably identifies him as a heavenly messenger. Sitting in the tomb, he, too, points offstage. This time, the message is 'He has gone ahead!' Once again the proper response is, of course, to follow: Jesus has gone into Galilee before them, and they must follow him there.

The dramatic force of this command is enormous. If the words of John the Baptist summoned *us*, as well as the inhabitants of Jerusalem, to follow the Coming One, the message of the young man at the tomb is surely addressed to us, as well as to the disciples. The stage play has become, in effect, an evangelistic rally! The evangelist points into the distance, assuring us that Jesus has gone ahead of us, and all we have to do if we want to see him is to follow. One by one we leave our seats, come down to the stage, and leave the theater.

The Final Word

If only Mark had stopped writing there, with that powerful summons to discipleship, everyone would surely have agreed that this was a powerful way to end a story. He has presented us with a challenge—to set out in faith—and left his readers to respond. But he follows it with verse 8, which brings us down to earth with a bump. At this stage, he tells us, the women lost their courage. They fled from the tomb in terror and said nothing to anyone, because they were afraid. And there he ends his narrative, leaving us puzzled and confused. Why?

We do not really like Mark's ending. Matthew and Luke clearly felt more was needed; so did John. All three recount appearances of the risen Lord. At an early stage, readers clearly felt that Mark could not have intended to end his gospel at verse 8, so various attempts were made to round the story off. They were hardly successful, but these attempts seemed to confirm the suspicion that Mark's gospel was incomplete. Commentators concluded either that Mark had never finished writing it, or that the ending had somehow been lost. Neither explanation is really convincing.

We do not really like Mark's ending. But *why* do we not like it? Is it not because we demand what we imagine is some kind of concrete evidence? We expect an appearance of the risen Christ, and Mark has given us only an empty tomb. We expect the witnesses of these great resurrection appearances to be disciples, and all we are given is the testimony of a few women—and who can believe what *they* say? Indeed, the women apparently failed to report what had happened! Surely, we think, Mark could not have intended to end his gospel without describing how the disciples met with Jesus, how they saw him, touched him, and received from him face to face the assurance that they had been forgiven? No wonder we find his ending unsatisfactory. No wonder we ask for more.

But are we right to do so? Is Mark perhaps, after all, a more profound theologian than us all? For what kind of "concrete evidence can he give us? The account of an appearance of Jesus to his disciples, perhaps? But why should that be any more persuasive than an empty tomb? To be sure, the women *could* have mistaken the tomb; and the disciples might well have experienced a hallucination when they thought they saw Jesus. We think the story should be "rounded off" by assuring us that the disciples did indeed go to Galilee, and that they saw Jesus there. What happened next, we want to know? How can Mark end his book without telling us? How can he break off in what seems like the middle of a sentence? How can he leave us without the certainty that what he is telling us about Jesus is true?

But how *can* we be certain that the good news about Jesus is true? Certainly not by relying on the testimony of others! Nor by expecting "concrete evidence." Had Mark given us an account of an appearance, we might have concluded that "seeing is believing." He, however, clearly believes that it is the other way round—that "believing is seeing." "Go," runs the message to the disciples, "follow Jesus to Galilee, and you will see him there." The first step, then, is to trust. It is as true for us as for the disciples: It is only by taking the step of faith for ourselves that we will see Jesus. "Are you the Messiah?" asked the high priest; "Are you the King of the Jews?" inquired Pilate; however, it is for *us* to decide whether he is or not. "Has he been raised from the dead?" we wonder, and once again it is we who must answer the question.

Mark is a true evangelist. He is writing for men and women who never met Jesus. The only way in which they will "see" Jesus is with the eyes of faith. How brilliant a strategy, then, to end his gospel, *not* with an account of the disciples seeing Jesus, but with a command to set out in faith. It is as though he were saying to us, "We are being asked to do what Jesus asked his disciples to do; to set out, trusting in him. It is only when they obeyed that they saw him, and it is only when *we* obey that we shall know him. 'Blessed are those who have not seen, and yet have believed.'"

But we still have not explained why Mark ends with the women's terror, flight, and silence. Interestingly, we again have links with the rest of the gospel. The words used concerning the women's emotions echo words used earlier in the story to describe human reactions to Jesus' miracles; it is hardly surprising if they feel awe and amazement when confronted with the greatest miracle of all! If they are afraid, that certainly indicates that they have not fully comprehended what has happened. Yet how *could* they? Their silence, too, reminds us of earlier occasions when Jesus *commanded* silence. Before his death and resurrection, the truth could not be fully comprehended or spoken about. Now the time has come to speak, and the women stay silent! This, too, is an indication they have not understood. They flee, just as the disciples fled from the Garden (14:40), another sign of failure! At the end of the story, even the stalwart women let Jesus down.

Surprisingly, Mark's final words are not, after all, a ringing challenge to us to believe, but an account of human failure—of incomprehension and disobedience. So how, we ask, was the good news ever passed on? If the women failed to deliver the message, did the disciples ever make their way to Galilee and meet the risen Lord? If not, why is Mark bothering to tell the story at all?

But, of course, we have the answer. He *is* telling the good news. And that means that somehow the message got through, though how he does not explain. Perhaps the women finally overcame their fear; perhaps Mark simply meant, "They did not say anything to anyone *else*"—apart from the disciples, that is.[10] By ending with the women's reaction, Mark reminds us of the importance of our response, and of the vulnerability of the gospel.

The good news is entrusted to a few women. "Outrageous," we say, or we *would* have said if we had been living then, for as they always say, "in the first century, women's testimony was totally disregarded!" What *was* God thinking of? They fail: what a ridiculous end to Mark's story. But think back again over the gospel. Has not the whole story been about divine power on the one hand, and human failure on the other? Up to this point in the narrative, the failures have, to be sure, been those of the *men* in the story; but now even the women have succumbed! We remember those various quotations from Isaiah, spelling out what happens when the people fail, when their hearts are hardened and they do not respond. Yet Isaiah 40 assured us that the Lord is here and that his paths are being made straight. Mark's story is of divine grace, but grace does not compel; men and women are free to respond or to refuse. We are confronted not only with divine power, but also with divine vulnerability. We can believe, or we can reject the good news. We can follow Jesus into Galilee, or we can turn away.

Mark does not give us what we expect: instead of an appearance we have a promise; instead of joy we have fear, instead of confidence we have flight. What he offers us is a challenge to trust and to obey the summons to follow Jesus. And he offers us the realization that, *in spite of all our failures, the good news cannot be defeated or destroyed.*

How do *we* preach Mark's gospel? We do not need to! Mark is himself the evangelist, the preacher of good news. All *we* need to do is to allow him to speak for himself.

5

Mark and Becoming Fully Human

FREDERICK D. AQUINO

What does it mean to be fully human in view of Mark's narrative? What shade of human selfhood emerges?[1] What implications materialize for the homiletical task? I bring these questions to the text, rather than allowing it to create such questions. However, theology calls for multifaceted reflection. In our attempt to read texts, and in this case an ancient one, we explore a world imagined by and projected beyond the world of the text. Serious writers envision a world beyond their own; the gospel of Mark certainly falls into this category.[2]

I couch the question of selfhood in the Markan schema of two logics: a thicker selfhood immersed in the logic of the kingdom of God or a thin selfhood restrained by the logic of survival. Mark contrasts these logics, thereby moving the concrete self from a narrow to a more expansive understanding of God, self, other, and world. However, my question of selfhood assumes that the interpretive path is neither ancient insulation nor hypercritical relevance. The gospel is neither a static deposit of timeless truths nor is it incapable of constructive promise under critical scrutiny. To simply transfer Mark's story to our own setting is equivalent to an uncritical download of isolated facts or demonstrated truths.

Its relevance lies not in facile connections between the past and present but in synthetic possibilities actualized by constructive and complementary insights.

As a result, the question of human selfhood shapes my reading of Mark. The competing logics of meaningfulness in Mark create a divided self that experiences a sense of alienation while considering a call to a fuller humanity. The kingdom of God unfolds a new, yet radical, way of thinking, feeling, and being in the world. Our perspectival glance expands into a different way of understanding relationships, power, property, and justice. The opposite tendency is to constrict the glance, pursuing business as usual. What we see in Mark is a profound and radical assessment of God incarnate and its implications for a self shaped by the logic of the kingdom. The location of what God is up to lies in the strangest of places, reconnecting people with the purpose for which God created them.

Thinking through Selfhood

The question of human selfhood comes in many forms. For example, one may employ the multidisciplinary lens of cognitive science, psychology, biology, philosophy, literature, and theology to decipher the meaning of human selfhood. I choose, however, a philosophical focus, mediated through the literary and theological world of Mark's gospel. Thus, I will not address the scientific aspects of human selfhood or pursue central questions in the philosophy of mind. This interdisciplinary probe is important, but will have to wait for another time and occasion. Perhaps my preliminary exploration will foster a broader conversation. In many ways my approach here resembles Paul Ricoeur's philosophical and literary construal of selfhood, tracing concrete possibilities of human selfhood and human action. This move seems appropriate, given the nature and setting of the 2005 Rochester Sermon Seminar and this volume.

The connection between text and self is not a one-to-one correlation or a full absorption into either world, but a complex and dynamic process. What surfaces is a dialogical conversation in which a "thickly populated" self enters a community of informed critics "who stand at different temporal and spatial removes."[3] Likewise, I approach the question of selfhood through "commitments and identifications" that furnish "the frame or horizon within which I can try to determine from case to case what is good, or valuable, or what ought to be done, or what I endorse or oppose."[4] To do otherwise is to experience disorientation or an identity crisis in which the self loses its frame of reference. As we shall see, Mark disrupts a particular frame of reference while inviting the self to pick up the pieces through a new way of being in the world. Rethinking self-definition comes through a web of interlocutors.

So the self discovers a way of being in the world through a network of commitments, perspectives, and values. From this stance, the self engages the hermeneutical issues, comparing particular experiences with other sources of informed judgment.[5] It draws conclusions in conversation with others. In this regard, Mark opens up a narrative possibility of being in the world, redefining the self's relation to God, neighbor, and world. The contours of human selfhood reflect such a communal process of discernment; this is not merely the outcome of isolated judgments, but rather a formative process of weaving "cares and commitments in which one is bound to become lost and to need the friendly and credible words of others in order to find one's way, in which at any time a choice may present itself."[6]

The gospel of Mark depicts human selfhood as an act of becoming, the manifestation of human possibility. The truthfulness of Mark's narrative is not measured merely in terms of verification or falsification, but rather in terms of manifestation—letting go and allowing a world of possibility to manifest itself.[7] What emerge hopefully are greater levels of understanding. In this sense the varied shades of human selfhood are deeply temporal, enmeshed in the contingencies of everyday experiences. Mark's narratival unveiling of the logic of the kingdom refigures new possibilities of understanding God, self, other, and world. Narratival existence is one way to refigure selfhood.

Looking through a Kingdom Lens

The logic of the kingdom of God in Mark connects discourse and way of life, redirecting how we should think and how we should live. It dissolves the distinction between thought and practice, challenging old homiletical paths. Proclaiming the good news implies a shift in thought and behavior. The message and embodiment of the kingdom are inextricably linked in the person of Jesus. He is paradigmatic for understanding the nature and scope of the kingdom of God and for understanding what it means to be fully human. We see God, self, neighbor, and world through the incarnation of God's reign in Jesus. From this perspective, we imagine a different way of understanding human life and the contours of human action. However, preaching is not merely an imaginative discourse about the nature of Jesus Christ; it fuses discourse and way of life and invites us to inhabit a way of being from and beyond the world of the text.

The kingdom of God, as a tensive symbol, rules Mark's story, thereby serving as the basis of Jesus' proclamation and activities. The synopsis of the kingdom in 1:14–15 undergirds the portrayal of characters, the depiction of events, and the form of life embedded in and projected beyond the world of Mark. "The time is fulfilled, and the kingdom of God has come near; repent, and believe in the good news" (Mk. 1:15). The narratival unfolding of the story is an expansion of this observation. Jesus is the new representative of God's reign. This squares with Mark's opening remarks that Jesus is the Son of God. The varied characterization in the story illustrates the inclusive nature of the kingdom and the dynamic, yet loaded, responses to proclamation and embodiment of the kingdom in Jesus' ministry. These characters provide a constructive link between the reader and the world of the text. The human soil is ripe for productivity and set for dehumanizing activity.

The brief account of the wilderness signals a shift in perspective. The setting of Jesus lying with "wild beasts" and the angelic service rendered to him grabs our attention (Mk. 1:13). A radical shift in orientation has occurred; God has curbed Satan's rule and has inaugurated the new age. Jesus also reveals the nearness of God's rule by calling, teaching, exorcising demons, and healing sick people (Mk. 1:16–45). Specific praxes follow proclamation of God's rule. Simon's mother-in-law serves as one example. After the disciples inform Jesus about her situation, he responds compassionately, restoring her health. She replies with a servant disposition (Mk. 1:31). Previously the angels served him, and now a person does.

Such a shift creates conflict; God's rule overturns all other powers and claims to authority, and the conflicts come to focus on Jesus, the agent of God's rule. In this regard, the kingdom shatters legal, purity, and social boundaries. Jesus' message engenders conflicts with established purity boundaries by inviting the impure and the socially marginal into the family of God (Mk. 1:21–24, 40–45; 2:1–17; 3:1–6). Human need takes precedence over oppressive distortions of God's primordial intentions for the created order (Mk. 2:23–28; 3:1–6). Induction into the new Jesus society requires obedience to God's will—following God's representative, Jesus. Those who malign Jesus and declare him "insane" remain outside the mysterious kingdom borders (Mk. 3:23–29, 31–35; 4:11–12).

The logic of the kingdom can be seen in three representative ways. First, the logic of the kingdom unfolds through the rhetoric of irony, illustrated in the dialectic of insider and outsider in chapters 4—8. Second, it surfaces in the theme of sight and blindness in chapters 8—10. Third, the logic of the kingdom of God expands the borders of human selfhood in chapter 11. There is more to the story, but I restrict the focus to these three areas.

Insider/Outsider
Deconstructed Expectations (Mark 4—8)

The mystery of the kingdom materializes in the theme of insider and outsider. We expect the disciples (insiders), who have been endowed with the mystery of the kingdom of God" (Mk. 4:11), to incorporate Jesus' kingdom perspective. The insider/outsider language echoes Isaiah 6:9, presupposing, at least in principle but not in fact, that "for those outside, everything comes in parables; in order that 'they may indeed see, but not perceive, and may indeed hear, but not understand; so that they may not turn and be forgiven'" (Mk. 4:11b–12, author's translation). However, the disciples exhibit inconsistent behavior. On one hand, they show loyalty and courage, "with a capacity for sacrifice, and perceptive enough to follow Jesus. On the other hand, they are afraid, self-centered, and dense, preoccupied with their own status and power."[8] In fact the disciples perceive Jesus' message of the kingdom of God as outsiders do. As the heirs of the kingdom of God, the disciples see, hear, and respond to Jesus' kingly demands as the blind, deaf, and hard-hearted. Our expectations of the disciples fall short of narrative resolution, forcing a reevaluation of what it means to pursue Jesus' kingdom vision. Alternatively, unexpected characters in the story contribute meaningfully to our perception of what it truly means to be a disciple in God's kingdom or what it means to be fully human.

Within the framework of 4:11—8:21, Mark leads us to see, hear, and understand that the kingdom encompasses those least expected to see, hear, and understand God's arrival in Jesus Christ. After three boat scenes and two feeding stories, the disciples' incomprehension astounds us (see Mark 4:35–41; 6:30–44, 45–52; 8:1–21). They still do not recognize Jesus as the master of the sea and bread-provider of the wilderness. God's rule is differentiated from what most characters in the story expect. Mark explains that their lack of perception stems from hardness of heart (Mk. 6:52; 8:17). Ironically, outsiders respond to Jesus' regal requirements like insiders (for example, the Gerasene demoniac, 5:1–20; the story of the hemorrhaging woman, 5:24b-34; the Syrophoenician woman, 7:24–30).

Just like a lamp, God's new order radiantly manifests itself and cannot remain hidden. Moreover, the kingdom's global borders extend to all the peoples of the earth (Mk. 4:21–32). Hence, Mark invites us to participate in the "confident assurance that, like the mustard seed, the kingdom of God [will] surely become the greatest of all kingdoms, embracing all the peoples of the world and empowering them to live under its protection and security."[9] In fact, Mark employs the verb *hear* to attune the reader to Jesus' parabolic discourse about the nature of God's new apocalyptic order. If they have ears, let them hear.[10]

Mark 4:11–12, therefore, illustrates the ironic nature of the mystery of the kingdom. A rhetoric of irony undergirds the portrayal of the disciples in 4:11–13 and in 8:17–21. Jesus reverses the language of 4:12 on the disciples: "Do you have eyes, and fail to see? Do you have ears, and fail to hear?" (Mk. 8:18). The question is whether the concrete self will think and behave as an insider, reflecting the values and commitments of the kingdom, or as an outsider, constricting the focus to business as usual. The answer is not as obvious as we might think, given how the contours of selfhood emerge under the reign of God.

Mark's message about the kingdom is not captive to any situation, calling all to accept God's vision and resist the temptation to rule the story. Do we struggle with this tendency in our preaching? The new order calls us to rethink power, boundaries, and ethnocentric tendencies. Discipleship echoes the dynamic nature of the kingdom; God's kingdom is for all nations (Mk. 11:17). Repentance is not to be confused with a list of negative rules, but instead signals a mind-set open to the activity of God's new order. What habits, practices, and environments help us to proclaim, discern, and embody the nearness of the kingdom?

Seeing Again (Mark 8—10)

Two narratives about blind men disclose a motif of blindness versus sight (Mk. 8:22–26; 10:46–52), forming an ironic tension between the blind men and the persistent blindness of the disciples. By means of three passion predictions, Jesus prepares the disciples for an agonizing journey to Jerusalem (Mk. 8:31; 9:31; 10:33–34). After each passion prediction, the disciples blunder and misunderstand Jesus' statements about his fate because they set their mind "not on divine things but on human things"(Mk. 8:33). We, like the disciples, need Jesus to touch us again. Fear, not faith, blinds our vision of God's apocalyptic reversal of expectations.

Seeing, hearing, and understanding the logic of the kingdom are not business as usual. After Jesus rebukes Peter's response to his first passion prediction and instructs the crowd about the meaning of discipleship, he makes an enigmatic statement about the kingdom of God: "Truly I tell you, there are some standing here who will not taste death until they see that the kingdom of God has come with power" (Mk. 9:1). Jesus has just instructed the disciples about the fate of the Son of Man. The cross is the path to understanding the nature of the kingdom of God; it involves rejection, betrayal, and denial.[11] Yet the disciples' comfort and fascination with mountaintop experiences (e.g., the gathering of Moses, Elijah, and Jesus in Mk. 9:2–8) miss the point. The sower will be crucified. The power of the kingdom will be revealed in a suffering Messiah.

By his actions and thoughts, Jesus represents God's new order. Moses, Elijah, and God confirm this insight. Accordingly, Mark challenges the self to follow Jesus "on the way" (Mk. 10:52). Elijah (John the Baptist) came clothed in camel's hair, and Herod killed him (Mk. 6:14–29). Jesus will be treated in the same way. Those who desire mountaintop experiences without a trip to Jerusalem fail to perceive the radical nature of the kingdom of God, namely, the call of discipleship, which entails a mode of courage in the face of suffering, persecution, and fear. The cross provides insight into the nature of God's rule and assures us that God will vindicate the community of the new age. Whoever courageously acknowledges the suffering Son of Man will stand with him, "when he comes in the glory of his Father with the holy angels" (Mk. 8:38).

The rhetoric of irony emerges again in the question of how one discerns (*idosin*) the power of the kingdom in the cross. Characteristic of the logic of survival, the scribes and chief priests (flat characters) tempt Jesus to come down from the cross so that they might "see [*idomen*] and believe" (Mk. 15:32). Ironically, their mockery unveils the mystery of God's rule. Without recognizing the nature of the kingdom of God, Jesus' opponents who scornfully "invest him as king" and "pay homage [actually] offer testimony of what [hearers/readers know] to be the truth."[12] The self, shaped by the logic of the kingdom, knows that Jesus is the Messiah, the incarnate reality of God's new order (Mk. 1:1, 15; 3:23–27). The splitting of the veil, the cosmic language, and the centurion's confession assure us that God's rule has come with power (Mk. 15:33–39).[13] We now experience God's reign through union with Jesus the crucified Messiah. His death reveals that "the old order has come to an end; it is a powerful symbol of God's eschatological rejection of evil as it operates in the world."[14]

Seeing again involves visualizing God's rule through Jesus' death (Mk. 13:1–26; 14:62; 15:33–39). We must die to self—become children—when we deal with family, wealth, and other members of the new order (Mk. 10:1–12, 17–22; 29–30).[15] We must boldly stand with Jesus, the suffering servant, and experience God's dynamic rule. Mark's hearers/readers, therefore, must soberly watch and endure until the end (13:1–2, 13–37). Let the hearers/readers understand (13:14). As the eschatological community, which gathers in the name of Jesus, Mark's hearers/readers realize that they now live between the cross and the future coming of the Son of Man (9:1; 13:26).[16]

How, then, do we cultivate the capacity to see the power of the kingdom? How does preaching reconfigure the community's self-understanding and its engagement with the world? What practices, people, symbols, and events form our understanding of human personhood? These questions presuppose an ethos of formation in which the self discerns the logic of the kingdom and its embodied expressions; the community cannot hide behind sacred cows or coping mechanisms.

A Kingdom of Inclusion (Mark 11)

The story of Bartimaeus concludes the blindness versus sight material and anticipates Jesus' Davidic journey through Jerusalem. With restored sight, Bartimaeus, unlike the disciples, follows Jesus "on the way" to Jerusalem (Mk. 10:52). Initially, Jesus' entry into Jerusalem may lead us to think that he has come to inaugurate the kingdom of God in the manner of a warrior king (for example, Zech. 14; Ps. 118:25–26). The focus shifts from nationalistic fervor ("Blessed is the coming kingdom of our ancestor David!" Mk. 11:10) to critique ("May no one ever eat fruit from you again," Mk. 11:14) and inclusion ("My house shall be called a house of prayer for all the nations," Mk. 11:17). The stories about the withering tree and Jesus' actions in the temple correct nationalistic presuppositions about the kingdom. Jesus is not the anticipated nationalistic Messiah, sanctioning the ideology of political revolutionaries. Rather, Jesus, the suffering Messiah, shows that the cross is the route through which we share in God's reign. This logic materializes in service, peace, and openness to the expansion of the kingdom.

Jesus, representing God's new order, reverses expectations. God's rule surpasses national boundaries and extends its borders to Gentiles and the socially marginalized: God's inheritance is now *"for all the nations,"* not a "den of brigands"(Mk. 11:17, author's translation). The critique of the triumphal entry and the inclusive prayer create conflict with temple authorities. Impressed with Jesus' answers to such authorities, a certain scribe approaches him with a question: "Which commandment is first of all?" The scribe concurs with Jesus' answer—wholehearted service to the creator and respect for the creation—but adds a statement of comparison: "and to love your neighbor as yourself is greater than all burnt offerings and sacrifices" (Mk. 12:33, author's translation). Acknowledging the scribe's prudent observation, Jesus replies: "You are not far from God's rule" (Mk. 12:34, author's translation). Jesus has the power to declare a person's nearness to God's new order. In the kingdom of God, orthodoxy and praxis are intertwined. One without the other misconstrues the heart of the new order.

Mark illumines the social dimensions of the new order. The community of cross-bearers loves, respects, and performs acts of devotion for her neighbors. The scope of the new order includes contact with Gentiles, leaders, the impure, the possessed, and lepers. The community expresses its love for God through service to others, not acts of impropriety. Unlike the scribes who wish to be endowed with special status and privileges, the new community finds identity in Jesus the crucified Messiah.

As Mark 11:1–24 indicates, the kingdom of God is open to all; prayer, service, and kindness link us to God and to one another. What are the contemporary challenges in reading and embodying this text in our preaching? Jesus roots his ministry in the twofold commandment of loving God and neighbor. What concrete strategies, practices, and environments help us materialize the twofold commandment today? How do we connect prayer, service, and inclusion? What does this posture look like today in our church and in surrounding communities?

Expanding the Self

Fundamental to these stories is a contrast of two logics of self-hood. The logic of the kingdom envisions an expansive human selfhood, while the logic of the old order defines authenticity in terms of status, wealth, power, and artificial boundaries. The logic of the old order is self-centered rather than other-centered. Fear, not faith, perpetuates the human fracture, assuming that human beings are created for Sabbath. The old order fails to see, hear, and understand the call to experience wholeness through submission and fundamental regard for the other. It forgets the basis of human well-being, namely, love for the Creator and for neighbor. The logic of the kingdom, by contrast, is not an annulment of our humanity, but rather a critique of a base level in which we define ourselves in terms of power, wealth, and status.

The focus on contrasting depictions of selfhood here fits with what John Zizioulas describes as the difference between "biological" and "ecclesial" existence.[17] Biological existence, from a minimalist perspective, perceives the self in terms of basic levels of survival and imagines this impulse as the only construal of human selfhood. Mark's narrative calls us to a fuller understanding of what it means to be human, perhaps analogous to the category of ecclesial existence—a community shaped by the logic of the kingdom. Power—mediated through acts of kindness, service, and submission—reflects the logic of the kingdom, though with the cross as a fundamental interpretive lens. Actualizing this call to a fuller humanity comes through the route to Jerusalem. Ecclesial existence is a natural consequence of biological existence. It moves from the logic of individualism to the logic of relationality, in which the self participates in the life of God, the only source of communal identity and life. Jesus is the paragon of what it means to be human, participating in the human situation (biological existence) and in the life of God (ecclesial existence).

Obviously Mark's narrative is not loaded with such an explicitly philosophical construal. Yet the two logics in Mark seem similar to the distinction between biological and ecclesial existence. The things of God entail sharing in the reign of God as a communal and collaborative enterprise, whereas the logic of the old order is self-absorption, hoarding goods, and setting out ethnocentric boundary markers. The logic of the kingdom presupposes that "God *and the world cannot be ontologically placed side by side as self-defined entities.* Creaturely truth is dependent upon something else, in which it participates; this is truth as *communion by participation.*"[18] Mark's story critiques insecure quests for status, power, and meaningfulness. People who embrace the logic of survival distort the meaning of being human, thereby creating conflict, oppression, and artificial boundaries.

Consequently, expanding the self in Mark involves crossing purity boundaries, redefining status, and reconfiguring the nature of community. It rethinks the connection between gospel and human potential. The link is the kingly vision of things, not the annulment of things. Proclamation of the coming kingdom is linked with the praxes of Jesus' ministry. Preaching, then, is not merely oral vestiges of the reality of God's reign but is a manifestation of its power in our midst. Perhaps, we need to see anew the power in our midst, as Mark 8—10 seems to imply about the lack of insightfulness on the part of the disciples (insiders). Another way of stating it is to see embodiment as collapsing the distinction between message and messenger. Preaching must echo the logic of the kingdom in its proclamation and embody its insights in our individual and collective persona.

The temptation to divorce person from message sounds Gnostic, especially given the fact that the mystery of the kingdom is heard in the proclamation of Jesus and seen in the activity of Jesus. In other words the nearness of the kingdom is not merely a disembodied word or the stringing together of homiletical moves. Rather, the nearness of the kingdom finds its locus in the gathering of disciples in a house and the anointing of Jesus in the house of a leper.

A fuller version of humanity is other-centered. From this perspective, the expansive nature of the kingdom fosters a thickly populated self, not an ethnocentric construal of faith-based victory dances. If anything, the shade of selfhood that emerges from Mark sees the corrosive power of narrow constraints or borders. It shows how the stance of self-importance materializes in abuse of power. The self here loves to be greeted in the markets, wants the best seats in the synagogue and at the banquets, and devours the house of widows (Mk. 12:38–40). For the expansive self, power is transformed into service. The logic of the kingdom does not lead to lording over people but rather to serving their needs (Mk. 10:42–45).

The cross serves as a fundamental symbol for expanded selfhood. The kingdom of God advances when the community takes up its cross, follows Jesus to Jerusalem, and bears witness to God's decisive act and rule in Jesus the Messiah, the Son of God. In spite of its present crisis, the community must open its house to all nations and extend its message to the oppressed, socially marginal, and unforgiven. The call to being fully human involves serving others, reconciling radically different groups, and showing true piety. In an age in which we are reducing our humanity to a collection of neurons or cells, the gospel of Mark calls for a thickly populated disciple, one immersed in helping people imagine the connection between our humanity and the twofold command. True religion, for Mark, is a human-enriching experience. Human well-being is the basis of understanding observance of the Sabbath (Mk. 2). The old logic trivializes doing "good" and "saving life" by subordinating them to legalistic observance of the Sabbath. Jesus places a high premium on human needs and challenges purity and political boundaries; will the contemporary reader hear and embody the logic of the gospel? The bottom line is that Jesus as authoritative interpreter of the Torah and as the lord of the Sabbath redefines the nature of community. Though ritual is important, it should not override the greater concern of human need. Incarnational preaching imagines a world in which the locus of ecclesial space moves from occupiers of God's prerogative to a "house of prayer for all the nations" (Mk. 11:17).

Preaching: Becoming Fully Human

The self that emerges in Mark is grounded in the contingencies and complexities of the world. Yet the narrative moves the self from the particular to the more comprehensive, pursuing the expansive logic of the kingdom and its implications for the question of human selfhood. The result is the formation of a thicker and more expansive self. Biological existence, though fundamental to our survival, is not enough. Becoming more "visible to oneself is a matter of becoming divided from oneself," and hopefully this process fosters greater understanding of what it means to be fully human.[19]

Expanding the concrete self involves something more than imagining the gospel; the call is to embody the way of life that you discourse. Thus, preaching is incarnational and dialogical. Connecting philosophical anthropology and preaching is extremely important here. The focus is on the kind of human selfhood that we might decipher both in Mark's narrative and in our context today. The interpretive process is complex and dynamic. The self is a dialogical reality, envisioning fresh ways to incarnate the logic of the kingdom of God. The network of interlocutors both in the text and in our contemporary experience helps us reframe priorities, goals, and proposals of human flourishing.

Preaching, then, must also become dialogical. Its interpretive gesture is incarnational, reflecting, deliberating, articulating, imagining, and fleshing out a particular way of being in the concrete moments of human existence. Our preaching reflects commitment to a particular framework. To deny this interpretive dimension is to strip the gospel of its flesh and join in the Gnostic proposal of a disembodied idea. In our case today, we preach to understand the logic of the kingdom and engage in the process of becoming fully human.

6

If Mark the Evangelist Could See Mel Gibson's *The Passion of the Christ*

JOHN BARTON

Karl Barth is often given credit for saying that one should prepare for preaching with a Bible in one hand and a newspaper in the other. If he actually said this, the statement must be understood with a certain amount of subtlety, given Barth's dialectical understanding of revelation. Nevertheless, the advice is good; and the point is simple: To preach well, we must know our world and know how to put scripture in dialogue with those influences and powers that shape the thoughts and experiences of our hearers. I suspect that if Barth were alive today, he might supplement his advice by saying that one should prepare to preach with a Bible in one hand, a newspaper in the other, and a video club card in the back pocket. In other words, film is one of those shaping influences in our world and has a significant influence on many of those who hear our preaching.

Mel Gibson's *The Passion of the Christ* was released on February 25, 2004. Beyond being the top-grossing R-rated movie of all time, it has proven to be one of the most remarkable events in the history of film, at least with regard to the specific impact on Christian thought and experience. While some of the media hype has passed, the influence of this film is far from over. In March 2005, *The Passion of the Christ, Recut* appeared in theatres intending to reach "new audiences." In addition, with a mix of aggressive marketing of the DVD, a large number of *Passion* resources, and religious zeal to match, the influence of the film has continued to spread around the globe. I have a number of connections in East Africa. Since the release of the VHS and DVD, the film's influence has even reached remote areas that require mobile, battery-powered equipment. For better or for worse, this film continues to directly shape and reflect an incredibly large number of people's understandings and mental images of the death of Jesus, as well as understandings and assumptions about the Christian message in general. As those who preach and teach, therefore, it is imperative that we continue to critically assess such influences as we go to scripture on behalf of our communities of faith. This essay will contribute to such an assessment by allowing the gospel of Mark to interact with the film at several levels.

Let me suggest the following verse as our entry way into our discussion: "And when the centurion, who stood there in front of Jesus, heard his cry and saw how he died, he said, 'Surely this man was the Son of God'" (Mk. 15:39).[1] This is an amazing moment in Mark's narrative, as commentators have often noted. This centurion provides us with the clearest and most complete statement of understanding about Jesus' identity in the gospel, even if he may have not been completely aware of the significance of his own statement. Furthermore, the statement is made possible only at the foot of the cross and precisely at the moment of Jesus' death. In other words, for Mark something about "how Jesus died" is critical for understanding Jesus, which in turn is critical for discipleship. An understanding of "how Jesus died" is also critically important to Mel Gibson. The entire film revolves around such a presentation. The pertinent questions for our consideration, then, are: How does the "how he died" of Mark 15:39 relate to the "how he died" of Gibson's silver screen portrayal? And what can we learn from this dialogue to help us better understand and faithfully preach the good news according to Mark?

Ducks and Rabbits:
Controversies Surrounding Gibson's Film

When reading the reviews and debates, it is striking how radically varied are people's descriptions, evaluations, and experiences of this movie. It seems that from this one film, many films have emerged. An illustration from the philosopher Ludwig Wittgenstein may be helpful here. In his *Philosophical Investigations,* Wittgenstein uses the now well-known duck/rabbit picture to consider issues of human perception and "seeing."[2]

The reality itself is what it is; the lines on the page don't move. Depending on how you look at the picture, however, you might see a duck or you might see a rabbit.

To further illustrate this, imagine a young girl who grew up in a community by a pond with many ducks. Since she saw ducks every day, and people in her community often spoke about the ducks, ducks were a part of life for the young girl. But the young girl never saw a rabbit or even a picture of a rabbit. No one in her community ever spoke about rabbits. If she were to look at this picture, she would only see a duck. In fact, she would not have the capacity to see the rabbit in the picture. That would not be a shortcoming on her part, but rather simply the result of her experience.

We learn from Wittgenstein that our experiences, which take place in communities, determine on some level our perceptions of the world. People can "look" at the same data, but "see" different realities. Some people are afraid that Wittgenstein's thoughts lead straight to epistemological relativism. But Wittgenstein is just trying to get us to observe what happens in the world.

Look, for example, at the debates over this movie. While everyone may be "watching" the same cinematic production, they are obviously not "seeing" the same film.[3] Some see the most beautiful and faithful portrayal of Jesus' death ever put to film. They see profound themes of suffering love and unbounded grace and victory and hope for all. For these viewers, the brutality of the film, while difficult to watch, is part of its beauty. Furthermore, these viewers find the "flashbacks" to be effective and powerful—such as when, in the middle of a brutal scene where Roman soldiers are beating Jesus, the film suddenly flashes back to Jesus teaching the crowds to "love your enemies and pray for those who persecute you." Many times, these viewers experience the film as an invitation to worship and devotion. Mel Gibson, they feel, has given the world a wonderful gift through this powerful movie.

In sharp contrast, others see a bloody testament to an archaic, medieval, and angry God. John Dominic Crossan calls the film Gibson's "Hymn to a Savage God."[4] A review in *USA Today* describes the film as "more gory than glory" and states that "*The Passion*'s hero is a man who preached love, but Gibson's movie is all about hatred."[5] Rather than creating devotion, these viewers see the film as the stuff of nightmares. Some sarcastically suggest better titles for the film might be *Mad Mel* or *Lethal Passion*.

Still others find in Gibson's *Passion* a Jesus to which the disenfranchised, the powerless, and the suffering people of the world can relate. Jim Wallis, despite his own reservations about the film, documents the reactions of a number of African American viewers who found the film moving and a refreshing change from the typical white, sanitized, European Jesus often portrayed in film. Robert Franklin adds that black communities, because of their experiences, have always been drawn toward Jesus as a suffering Savior and as one unjustly condemned by corrupt authorities and a corrupt system.[6] A Ugandan friend recently saw the film and said, "It is so touching and reminds us of the pains that we've seen people going through and even felt ourselves."

Probably the most widely known controversy concerns those who see the film as anti-Semitic, or, as Thomas Wartenberg describes it, "an anti-Semitic tract made by the son of a Holocaust denier."[7] This is a perspective that many Christians, because of differences in experience, simply do not understand (remember the duck/rabbit). Much could be said here that would be beyond the scope of this essay, but it is important to acknowledge that such critics—at least the good ones—are not merely concerned about being politically correct. These critics are concerned that the movie's treatment of Jews contributes to an environment that could result in actual acts of violence against Jews. They remind us of how history is littered with examples of such incidents surrounding anti-Semitic dramatizations of the passion. In 1539, for example, the Roman municipal authorities had to cancel the annual passion play after Christian audiences had angrily ransacked Jewish ghettos following the previous performance.[8] Hitler promoted the passion plays, stating, "Never has the menace of Jewry been so convincingly portrayed."[9] Furthermore, a number of Muslim countries have lifted bans on showing Hollywood films specifically so that *The Passion* could be shown in those countries. Apparently, these Muslim countries have accepted the movie not for its depiction of Jesus, which is obviously not in line with Muslim ideas, but for its depiction of Jews.[10]

There are so many conflicting perspectives and many things to think about and discuss. For this essay, I wish to bring the author of the earliest gospel into the discussions. What perspectives would Mark offer that would help us further evaluate Gibson's movie and our different experiences of it, as well as our understandings and experiences of the Christian message in general?

What Mark Reminds Mel (and Us) about Distance

Imagine Mark the evangelist and Mel Gibson sitting in a theater together watching and discussing this film. Elsewhere in this volume, professor Hooker asks us to imagine being in Mark's world in a first-century house or amphitheater. For this essay, I am asking us to reverse that to imagine Mark in our world. Trying to imagine this is a highly speculative undertaking that requires significant historical imagination! I think this imaginative exercise has more to offer than is immediately obvious.

Sara, my wife, and I lived in the East African country of Uganda for a number of years. We had the sometimes humorous privilege of introducing elements of the modern world to rural Ugandans who had never traveled outside their simple rural village. Sara traveled on a bus into a Ugandan city with a group of rural women, some of whom had never had such an experience. As the bus would screech around turns, and start and stop at intersections, the women—many of whom were 40 years old or older—would all hold tightly onto the seats in front of them, lean heavily into the turns, and scream and laugh as if they were on a roller coaster. Later that day, the same group came to stay at our house in a modern Ugandan town for a few days. In orienting the women to all of the modern gadgets around our house, Sara felt it necessary to give the group a brief introduction to the bathroom facilities. With the women all crammed into the bathroom, Sara flushed the toilet in demonstration. All the women leaned in to watch the water go down. Just as the water reached the bottom of the bowl and the toilet gave its last little gurgle, the women immediately broke out into applause and loud cheers. In fair turn, the Ugandans often had fun with us as we experienced elements of their world for the first time: trying to catch a chicken or balance a water jar on my head or learning the subtleties of a certain Ugandan vocational activity. In short, our abilities to understand different experiences and phenomena result from a lifetime of certain kinds of what Wittgenstein calls "training" (*Abrichtung*).

Now imagine Mark sitting next to Mel in a modern theater while being introduced to this film. Consider the incredible expanse of time and culture and language that would have to be traversed to make such an event possible. Mark would have so much to overcome. Even if all could be overcome and Mark was able to watch and understand the film for what it is technologically, think of how totally unprepared he would be to comprehend some of the thematic and cinematic elements of *The Passion*. Consider the following examples:

1. What would Mark think of the androgynous Satan figure with its hooded cloak (a cloak that resembles the one worn by the Evil Emperor in the Star Wars series, a cinematic sign of evil that we are all "trained" to understand). What would Mark think as this figure mysteriously moves in the crowds? What would Mark think of the scene in which a maggot is seen coming from Satan's nose? Would Mark be able to understand or even identify this figure?

2. For another horror-film–type example, how would Mark experience the group of Jewish children in the film who are laughing and playing around Judas and then suddenly morph into Stephen King-type demons and torment him?

3. Would Mark be able to follow the twelve flashbacks in the film and the way they are interwoven into the movements of the narrative to break up the long segments of brutality and give the events some "backstory?"

4. Would Mark comprehend the mood-setting elements such as that of the opening scene, in which the Garden of Gethsemane is portrayed less as a garden and more as a mysterious, foggy medieval forest, supplemented by eerie music and surround-sound audio effects?

5. Would Mark pick up on the scene near the end of the film where the "tear of God" falls from heaven at the moment of Jesus' death and sets into motion the reported earthquakes?

These are simply examples of the artistic expression used to enhance the film's message for those who are properly trained to perceive them. Other more significant thematic features of the film would be equally as removed from Mark's experience and knowledge. Consider the influence on the film of medieval passion plays and their intense focus on the last hours of Jesus' life; the film's narrative organization around the classic Stations of the Cross; Catholic characterizations of Mary the mother of Jesus[11]; and visual "quotes" in the film of famous works of art such as Michelangelo's *Pieta*. Many of these elements are lost on non-Catholic viewers in general.

Mark would also need to be introduced to Gibson's heavy reliance on the early nineteenth-century German nun Anne Catherine Emmerich. Emmerich was well known for her mystical dreams and visions of Jesus published after her death in 1824 as *The Dolorous Passion of Our Lord Jesus Christ*.[12] Emmerich's profound influence on the film is especially reflected in two elements: the detailed brutality of the crucifixion events and the antagonistic and even demonic roles of many of the film's Jews.

Here's the point: Through Mark's eyes, we receive a general reminder of the distance between the world of this film and the world of the author of the earliest gospel. At one point, Gibson stated his hope that watching the movie would be like "traveling back in time and watching the events unfold exactly as they occurred."[13] I have to wonder if trying to explain all the above elements to Mark in our imaginary dialogue would cause Gibson to reconsider such sentiments.

Of course, the reminder of distance should not stop with Gibson. Through this dialogue, we also are challenged to acknowledge our own distance from the text. In sermon preparation, we, like Gibson, are shaped by our histories. We consult a number of nonbiblical sources, and we employ artistic expression. We make choices using our abilities to reason and imagine; we employ contemporary humor and illustrations; and sometimes we even organize PowerPoint slides or use film clips. We stand in a pulpit or roam around a stage with a wireless microphone pinned to our clothes or wrapped around our ear. We read from leather-bound copies of the translation of our choice and speak to people in padded pews or folding chairs with their own leather-bound copies of scripture. After services, we go out to eat and then go home to watch a game. Can we imagine a world more distantly removed from the world Mark knew and to which he wrote his gospel? This is not a criticism of Mel Gibson or us. It is just a reminder, through Mark's eyes, of our distance, a reminder that will actually serve us well if we embrace it.

The dialogue between Mark and Mel, however, has more to offer us than just a reminder of distance. The discussion also turns to questions of message, starting with the question of whether Gibson is guilty of giving a distorted portrayal of Jesus.

"Who Do You Say I Am?": Is Gibson's Jesus the Jesus of Scripture?

In 1804, this country's third president assembled what has come to be called the *Jefferson Bible*. With a twist on Barth's advice, Thomas Jefferson sat in the White House in February of that year with several Bibles in one hand and a pair of scissors in the other. He cut verses and pasted pieces together to produce his own version of a gospel. Jefferson's Gospel presented a Jesus more compatible with Jefferson's worldview than was the Jesus of the four gospels. As an Enlightenment rationalist and deist, Jefferson could not bring himself to accept the Jesus of signs and wonders; but he did embrace Jesus' great ethical teaching and moral example. So when Jefferson's scrapbooking party was over, he had his own tailor-made gospel and a Jesus created in his own image: a rational ethicist void of any miracles or supernatural occurrences. (The cutting out of supernatural occurrences, by the way, included the cutting out of the resurrection. If you think Mark's short ending is odd as the women flee from the empty tomb in fear and remain silent about what they had seen, then consider a gospel that just leaves Jesus in the tomb.)

In a provocative article entitled "Jesus Nation, Catholic Christ," Stephen Prothero accuses Mel Gibson of being guilty of the same crime as Jefferson.[14] Gibson's Jesus-of-choice, however, is quite different than Jefferson's, according to Prothero. For Gibson, Jesus is primarily a "man of sorrows," a suffering Jesus filtered strongly through the medieval Catholic lens described above. This Jesus, the article says, is violently thrust into our faces in scene after brutal scene. Prothero further states that Gibson's portrayal is, in part, a reaction against still another uniquely American Jesus: the friendly, soft, Mister Rogers–type, "what a friend we have in" Jesus. (Another commentator describes this soft Jesus by imagining Barney the Dinosaur singing, "I love you/ You love me/ Let's be friends in Galilee." This mental image has caused me to lose some sleep in recent weeks). In other words, according to Prothero, Gibson seeks to replace a wimpy cultural "buddy Jesus" with a shocking medieval "bloody Jesus." Prothero summarizes these three invented, tailor-made versions of Jesus in the following way: *The Jefferson Jesus* is about the mind, and he came to earth to deliver moral maxims; the *Mister Rogers Jesus* is about the heart, and he came to earth to exude sympathy; and *Mel Gibson's Jesus* is all about the body, and he came to earth to, as Prothero "delicately" puts it, "spew blood."

Prothero's analysis is insightful and challenging. It demands attention in the context of a world in which Jesus is often shaped to fit some agenda and has been cast as, among other things, "black and white, gay and straight, a socialist and a capitalist, a pacifist and a warrior, a civil rights activist and Ku Klux Klansman." The pertinent questions include: Is Gibson really guilty of the same kind of cut-and-paste Jesus-creating as Thomas Jefferson? Is there a difference between what each has done? What are the implications for what each of us does every time we stand up to preach?

Of course, Mark knows something about the tailor-made–Jesus business. He had heard too many stories from Peter about his struggle with such issues. You can almost hear Jesus rebuking Peter: "Get behind me, Satan!" and, "You do not have in mind the concerns of God, but merely human concerns," and, "Whoever wants to be my disciple must deny themselves and take up their cross and follow me." Seeking to understand the words in the context of Mark's narrative, I think Jesus was telling Peter: "Peter, your cut-and-paste version of me will not do. In fact, something about it is demonic. But it's a start. I can still work with it. Now stay with me on the road, and we will continue to transform you and your images of me."

I think Mark would suggest that it is not enough for Prothero to merely accuse Gibson or any one else of inventing the Jesus they desire. It is not even enough to back this charge by highlighting what many consider to be the overly brutal or anti-Semitic portions of Gibson's film. With reference to these elements from the film, one can almost hear Mark's Jesus rebuke Gibson and say, "Get behind me, Satan!" But it seems to me Mark's primary question for Gibson and for us would not be concerning whether we are guilty of the tendency to create Jesus in our own image. Such a question would be hypothetical—we all are guilty. *Every time we preach, we are in danger of this.* Mark might rather ask, "Are you 'on the way?'" and, "Are you on the road with Jesus as he travels to Jerusalem?" and, "Are your self-created images of Jesus, *even ones with demonic tendencies,* continually being challenged and transformed as you journey with him on the way?" This seems to align with what Fred Aquino says in this volume about Mark's view of human nature as a dynamic process of "becoming," and Morna Hooker's exposition of the Markan theme of continually returning to Galilee (see Mk 16:7).[15] Are we on the way? These are questions we might not be able to answer for Mel, but we should take it to heart for ourselves.

Nevertheless, it is still important to ask whether we, despite our partial perspectives and limited abilities, are being faithful to scripture. How do we determine that? Similarly, despite its flaws, is Gibson's movie a faithful signpost to Jesus? We may not have any straightforward answer to that, but issues of accuracy are certainly part of the puzzle, so we now turn to those.

How He Died:
Biblical Accuracy or Hollywood Heroics?

An early report said Pope John Paul II, after seeing the film, simply stated, "It is as it was." Those close to the Pope later denied the report,[16] but it still brings to the surface the question of the film's accuracy. While Prothero considers Gibson's account an historical fabrication that tells us more about Mel than about Jesus of Nazareth, others defend the film on the grounds of what they claim to be its historical and theological accuracy. An Evangelical leader said, "this film is probably the most accurate film historically than anything that's ever been made in the English world...We were watching it for biblical accuracy and we thought it was as close as you can get."[17] A Vatican Cardinal adds, "Mel Gibson not only closely follows the narrative of the Gospels...[but is] faithful to the meaning of the Gospels, as understood by the Church."[18] An Anglican Cardinal even says, "I am ready to exchange all of my homilies on the passion of Jesus for just one scene from Mel Gibson's film."[19] It would be difficult to exaggerate the confidence these statements express for the accuracy and value of the film.

Obviously, not all agree that the film is so accurate historically or valuable theologically. Historically, some of the debate centers on whether the brutality the Jesus figure endured in the film is realistic. In April 2005, Frederick Zugibe published a revised edition of *The Crucifixion of Christ: A Forensic Inquiry.*[20] Zugibe is a forensic pathologist and medical examiner, as well as a practicing Catholic. The book was not written as a response to Gibson, but Zugibe does devote a few pages to Gibson's film and the question of its accuracy. His verdict is that the portrayal of the passion events in the film is, from a forensic perspective, far beyond reality. The flogging and scourging scene alone would have been beyond what any normal person could endure.

Of course, some defenders of the movie might immediately retort with, "Yes, but Jesus wasn't a 'normal person!' That's the whole point!" But is that the whole point? One wonders if Jesus' miraculous endurance and defiance in the face of overwhelming odds is part of the biblical message or simply the kind of Hollywood heroics that one could find in Sylvester Stallone movies, or in Gibson's own *Braveheart, The Patriot,* or even *Lethal Weapon.* In other words, for Jesus' death to be effective, must he have experienced superhuman torture and been able to endure that torture in a superhuman way?[21] I think Mark would consider such an assumption odd. But it does bring us back to the question of the centurion's confession. What *is* the significance of the statement, "And when the centurion...saw how he died..." (15:39), in Mark's gospel?

The gospel of Mark, while clearly portraying the crucifixion as a brutal event, gives fairly scant details. What the gospel account accomplishes in a few sentences Gibson's film projects into two hours of meticulous detail. Gibson claims that his primary sources were the four gospels and that he filled in the "details" from extra-biblical sources (most notably Emmerich's visions). When asked whether the amount of gore in the movie was necessary, for example, he responded, "That's just what's in the Gospel. I know how it went down."[22] He told Diane Sawyer in an ABC interview, "You know, critics who have a problem with me don't really have a problem with me and this film. They have a problem with the Four Gospels. That's what their problem is."[23] I imagine that Mark, however, would suggest that the opposite is actually closer to the truth: that a somewhat convoluted mixture of the four gospels provide the general structure and some details for the film, but that the extra-biblical materials are primarily responsible for shaping its overall ethos.

On the other hand, it seems obvious that the suffering that Jesus endured is significant to Mark as well. On this Mark and Mel would find some agreement. Mark portrayed Jesus as being "deeply distressed and troubled" (Mk. 14:33) and "overwhelmed with sorrow" (14:34). Jesus prays that the cup be taken from him, and his friends disown him. His executioners "condemned him as worthy of death," "spit at him," "blindfolded him," "struck him with their fists," "beat him," "bound him," "flogged [him]," "wove a crown of thorns and set it on him," "struck him on the head," and then "led him out to crucify him."[24] Certainly something about the suffering and brutality and sorrow that Jesus experienced is part of the "how he died" that is significant to Mark. One fascinating way to think about these aspects of Jesus' death is to compare them to those of the death of Socrates. His death sentence was carried out in a "civilized" manner, with Socrates confidently and calmly accepting and embracing his fate.[25] Whatever else can be said about the death of Jesus, it was not calm or civilized. While Jesus embraced his purpose in submission to God's will, he did not do so without a great amount of sorrow and suffering.

Nevertheless, it seems to me that Mark's emphasis is not on the details of how *brutally* Jesus suffered as much as it is on *who* is enduring *this kind of* suffering and *why*. Elsewhere in this volume, David Keller highlights the fact that Mark seems to avoid giving the brutal details of the crucifixion. "It's almost as if," Keller suggests, "Mark wants us behind the cross, not able to see what happens when someone is crucified."[26] In contrast to Gibson's detail, Mark directs his presentation by simply saying, "And they crucified him" (15:24). Keller's sermon also directs us to the consequent question: If Mark is not drawing attention to the brutal details, to what is he wishing to draw our attention?

Several years ago in Uganda, Sara and I came upon an angry mob brutally beating a man caught in a criminal act. Watching another human being pummeled in such a way was disturbing, to say the least. But many Ugandans, even kind and gentle Ugandans, consider such an event reasonable *since the attacked person was a thief*. Many consider such incidents to be deserved, public, and shameful forms of punishment that would be horrific for most people, but appropriate for a thief. Whether one agrees with such an idea or not, the point is that for Mark, it is not that the brutality Jesus endured was more severe than what others endure, but that the brutality was *shameful*, that which was seen as only appropriate for a common thief. A few weeks ago after seeing the film, an older Ugandan Christian woman—who undoubtedly had Ugandan examples of mob justice for criminals on her mind—commented, "Why would *this* happen to our Savior?"

Why, indeed? Those who preach from Mark cannot ignore this question. Why, according to Mark, did Jesus die?

Why He Died:
Gibson's "Canon within the Canon"

As mentioned earlier, many feel that Gibson's portrayal distorts the message of scripture beyond recognition. The film's focus on the last few hours leading up to Jesus' death is emphasized, some argue, to the message-damaging neglect of his life and ministry.

Such critics feel that the twenty-three-second clip of the Sermon on the Mount, for example, gets completely eclipsed by the almost two hours of crucifixion brutality. Other complaints point to the film's extremely brief, just over a minute, portrayal of the resurrection. Some experience the scene as an almost-forgotten, tag-on-at-the-end scene. And this is the event Christian theology often considers the central element of the story, an element without which the whole passion narrative is rendered impotent.

One must also consider what critics see as Gibson's overall theological approach or paradigm centering on "satisfaction" or "substitution" theories of the atonement. Such theories understand Jesus as taking onto himself the punishment that our sin requires. "He paid a debt I could not pay," is Gibson's major theological paradigm, one that for him is very intentional and personal. Gibson wants to highlight the fact that Jesus took *his* place, that *his* sin is responsible for Jesus' death, and that the same is true for all of us. He uses what is often considered one of the classic substitution passages from Isaiah 53 (a passage familiar to Mark's gospel as well) as the opening quote for the movie: "He was wounded for our transgressions...and by his wounds we are healed" (v. 5, author's translation). Gibson represented this conviction by insisting that his own hands be shown as the hands of the Roman soldier driving the nails into Jesus.

Critics say it is problematic to focus exclusively on satisfaction theologies to the neglect of other key theological themes in scripture such as the kingdom of God, the work of the Holy Spirit, the process of sanctification, the call of discipleship, the meaning of the resurrection, and many others mostly or totally absent from the film.[27] In other words, we can't just focus on being forgiven and ransomed and "getting saved" to the neglect of all else. As Dallas Willard has commented (although not in response to Gibson's film), this kind of emphasis creates "vampire Christians" who want Jesus Christ for his blood and nothing else.[28] James Martin specifically applies such concerns to the film:

> If one wishes to communicate the message of Jesus, one must proclaim the *full* message—which includes his revolutionary teachings, his astonishing miracles, his intimate relationships...his bold proclamation of the Kingdom of God and, most importantly, his resurrection.[29]

But Mark the evangelist might ask James Martin, "What does it mean to say that if one wishes to proclaim the message of Jesus they must proclaim the *full* message?" Is that possible every time we proclaim? If a partial message equals a distorted message, then we as preachers distort the message every time we open our mouths. Authors of the New Testament gospels know as well as anyone that one must be selective in making any presentation about the Christ. After all, as another evangelist once wrote, Jesus did many things and if all of them were written down it might fill the whole world with books (Jn. 21:25).

I can almost hear Mark empathizing with Gibson concerning the criticisms he has received over the short abrupt resurrection scene. "Don't worry, Mel," he might say, "You can't win with critics. They didn't like *my* short ending either. I even hear that others added to my ending later and even tried to spice it up with snake handling and poison drinking. They missed the point of my shorter ending! But I can say that if you need some encouragement on this issue, look up a certain professor named Morna Hooker. She at least understands what we are *trying* to do!"

As for criticisms of Gibson's narrow focus on satisfaction theories, Mark might ask: "Why should we require the film to represent all atonement theories equally?" Even the gospels do not do that. Mark highlights self-abandonment and discipleship far more than satisfaction, which overtly appears in only two verses: Mark 10:45 and 14:24. In other words, Mark reminds us that the "full" message does not come from a single movie, or a single sermon, or a single person, or even a single inspired gospel. The full message is embodied in the community of God as the Spirit empowers that community, and it lives and grows within the diversity of scripture (which is, it seems to me, a great plug for biblical preaching). In his better moments, Gibson knows the film's purposes are, at best, narrow:

> The film...is not meant as a historical documentary, nor does it claim to have assembled all the facts...It is not merely representative or merely expressive. I think of it as contemplative in the sense that one is compelled to remember...in a spiritual way which cannot be articulated, only experienced.[30]

Conclusions

So much more could and should be said. We have left many loose ends, and many rabbits—and ducks—that we could chase. Let me bring it back one last time to the preaching of Mark.

In college, I had the privilege to hear the preaching of Mike Cope every Sunday. Many know Mike and his ability to bring scripture to life in a transforming way. One Sunday he was preaching about the cross from the book of Mark and referenced the hymn, "When I Survey the Wondrous Cross." This wonderful song draws our attention and contemplative focus to the cross. It is also a personal favorite and has touched me deeply on a number of occasions. On that Sunday while preaching on the Markan call of discipleship, however, Mike observed that at some point we need to stop talking about the cross, stop singing about it, stop contemplating it, stop surveying it. Instead, we need to climb up on the thing. That observation is with me almost twenty years later. Homiletically, Mike used the hymn against itself, in a sense. That doesn't take anything away from the power of the hymn or the ability to use it positively. In this instance, however, Mike used it creatively (against itself) to bring to light *Mark's* message of the cross.

Personally, I do not have much interest or desire to view *The Passion of the Christ* again anytime soon. However, as long as the film remains a force in our world, shaping people's ideas of Christ and his death, then I think preachers can and should engage it. Those who preach can use it in a number of different legitimate and potentially powerful ways. Sometimes we may be able to reference the film positively—in line with the intended message— to dramatically illustrate what Jesus did "for us." We could, for example, have people imagine *their* hand pounding the nails instead of Gibson's hand. Or we could reference the brutality of the film and set it in relief, as the film does, with references to Jesus' command to "love your enemies and pray for those who persecute you."

At other times, however, we may use the film against itself to bring to light something in scripture beyond the intentions of the movie. Can we, for example, use *The Passion* to emphasize Markan discipleship? What if we imagined Gibson replacing the Isaiah 53 quote at the beginning of the film with Mark 8:35: "For whoever wants to save his life will lose it, but whoever loses his life for me and for the gospel will save it"? Such a change significantly recasts the film. Can we help our hearers imagine and think through the implications of such a recasting? Or what if, during a grueling scene during which Jesus is dragging the cross through the streets of Jerusalem, the film flashes back to Jesus teaching his disciples on the way, "Whoever wants to be my disciple must deny themselves and take up their cross and follow me" (8:34 author's translation)? Furthermore, can we imagine the scene in the theaters after *this* film was shown? I imagine that instead of theaters full of people touched and expressing sorrow and gratitude for a paid debt, the crowd's demeanor after *this* film might more reflect Mark 10:32: "...and the disciples were astonished, while those who followed were afraid." Should that describe what the scene in our churches might be like after we faithfully preach Markan discipleship? Astonished and afraid? This is unsettling, but it also seems to be in line with the idea that Fred Craddock and Tom Long and other homileticians have promoted for years. The preacher should say what the text says and do what the text does.

Finally, I imagine Mark ending the dialogue imagined in this presentation by turning away from Mel and the movie and turning toward us: the ones who preach his gospel. What would he say to us before being transported back to his world? I imagine him challenging us to embody the text that we preach with what we say and who we are. I imagine him challenging us to preach and live in such a way that the "Roman centurions" of the world can "see how we die to self" and therefore have the opportunity to proclaim, "Surely, Jesus is the son of God." Is that what people see in us? Does our preaching provide that opportunity?

7

The End Is Performance

Performance Criticism and the Gospel of Mark

RICHARD F. WARD

In the beginning was the performance; not the word
alone, not the deed alone, but both, each indelibly
marked with the other forever.

JOHN DOMINIC CROSSAN

A Scene in the Seminary Classroom

You are sitting in your first seminary class in New Testament listening to your professor tell you how these texts came to be. "Swirling around these written texts are lively, vital, and contested oral traditions," the professor says. "Resonances of those traditions are evident in the forms and patterns of writing and organization." You write that down in your notebook, certain it will show up on the exam. The professor continues, "Because these traditions are oral, they are lost in Christian memory. We cannot know how these traditions were spoken, presented, or performed. Were they chanted? Were they told as stories? Sung as hymns? They had no tape recorders or video cameras back then. Only the technology of writing preserved and shaped the early church's interpretations and meanings of the life, ministry, death, and resurrection of Jesus of Nazareth. Of this we can be certain. These texts were written to be heard through the act of reading aloud," the professor claims. But your mind drifts off. You wonder: "What would it have been

88

like to have heard these texts? Seen who was presenting them? Experienced them for the first time? Who was there? What was the setting? How did they sound?"

It is hard to hold that image in your mind because the scene blurs and you don't know how to fill in the details. Nothing in your experience is quite like it. You recall that your primary experience of reading has been in silence. Read orally, texts seem to flatten. Still you try to hold the image as best you can because you sense that how these texts were experienced was very important to those first hearers of these traditions. Otherwise, why would they have taken the step of writing them down? A question forms in your mind. You write it down in your notebook: What difference would it make in our experience and understanding of these texts today to know how they might have been performed then?

Performance Criticism: A Lively Art

The questions about biblical texts, their formation, articulation, and transmission are questions for an emergent discipline called "performance criticism."[1] At first, the word *performance* might put you off. Immediately, a cluster of negative associations gather around that word. It is easy to think first about its pejorative uses. You wonder how a term like "performance" can be taken seriously when it comes to biblical interpretation? Performance has to do with sham and pretense, right? Whenever you want to demean or devalue public behaviors you believe are inauthentic, you borrow from the vocabulary of theater. "That was too 'showy'!" you might say. Or, "She was just playacting to get her way!" Or, "It was all an act!" Pejorative uses of the word *performance* dominate our talk about human behavior, especially our talk about preaching. After all, preaching is about telling the *truth*! What does truth have to do with performance? Everything. *Performance,* in its most general sense, describes the execution of an action. In its most literal sense, *performance* means "carrying through to completion." Thought, intention, and action are inextricably bound and culturally situated within the matrix of social interaction. When thought is completed in action, performance results.

Many times, performance has something to do with *texts*— those found in books, stories, and plays, of course, but also those *scripts* our culture gives for the many social *roles* we play. In the happiest of circumstances, congruity and coherence happen as we enact our roles. Yet the "play" (as in the theater) often leads to conflict, divided loyalties, confused priorities, and experience of self that is multifaceted but fragmented and frustrating. Such is the stuff of artful expression—art imitates life. Christian theology teaches us of an irreducible "Self" known by God and sensed by others in our interactions. We bring that "Self" in all of its mystery to God in the prayers we perform, whether privately or corporately. *Prayer is an enactment of our relationship with God.* "Self" is reflected in the performance of the roles we assume. Through an array of "performances," the truth of who we are is realized, interpreted, transformed, and reconstituted.

How does a "performance critic" help us become lively readers, interpreters, and preachers of texts from Mark? Does the "performance critic" show up in the balcony ready to evaluate and critique how well we are performing our roles as preacher, interpreter, or human being? No. The performance critic appears within the enterprise of biblical interpretation to help us understand the entire complex of processes associated with the creation, transmission, and communication of our sacred texts. She or he invites us to understand these processes as part of an engaged and embodied interpretation that calls for a greater investment of intellect and imagination.

Performance Criticism Interpreted

The performance critic's entrance comes at a good time in the history of our contested but familial relationship with scripture. We live in a time when the rapid rise of electronic technologies has radically transformed the ways we communicate, process information, and internalize and embody knowledge. Even the traditions of public reading and interpretation are shifting into practices we are only beginning to understand. It is apparent that conventions of oral reading that served a culture when print was the dominant media are losing their capacities to communicate a text effectively. Listeners do not pay attention when a reader, who cares little for the communication of meaning or for the authority of a text, attempts to give it voice in the assembly in which biblical authority can no longer be generally assumed. How long has it been since a biblical text as read aloud held your attention? Biblical texts are being chanted again, recited from memory, even flashed up on large screens to incite renewed interest. Groups formed for the preparation of lectors within churches receive renewed attention. Such practices open new futures for the biblical texts by remembering past performance practices. The performance critic notes well how these changes are occurring and wonders what the relationship might be between these practices and the performance traditions that gave us these scriptures.

The "hermeneutics of play,"[2] which stresses dramatic enactment, role-playing, and recitation, has made significant impact on the study of scripture. "Playing" with the text comes to grips with the *orality* of scripture and aims to contribute to a transforming, experiential knowledge of a biblical text that resonates with the lived experience of our ancestors in faith. Performance criticism is a discipline of inquiry that arises out of these impulses and puts them together into a coherent strategy for "reading," interpreting, and communicating not only *what* scripture says, but also *how* it says it. Performance criticism even questions a text's identity! Is it strictly that set of words that now sit fixed and silent on a page, or is that text an "arrested utterance"[3] or a "moment in a dialogue" that has been transformed into writing? What we say about scripture and how it is designed to speak impacts our habits of reading, interpretation, and communication. To say that a biblical text belongs in the world of sound and not simply fixed in print changes the way we read and interpret it.

Not only does performance criticism help us communicate the texts, it also takes seriously the cultural contexts in which speakers and listeners alike first experienced the texts. When the interpreter of a text becomes its performer through conventions of speech and enactment, he or she loosens a text from its moorings in print and opens new dimensions for interpretation. The performance critic looks at the historical record and sees that "an encounter with these [biblical] texts has over and over again brought on unforeseen, creative events in the lives of those who enter it with an open mind."[4] Here then is the claim of this chapter: *performance criticism uncovers fresh material for interpretation of the text of Mark's gospel and leads to transforming experiences of reading the gospel for preaching and proclamation. By taking "performance" seriously in the transmission of gospel traditions, performance criticism gives us significant clues to how the gospel texts are to be preached and performed in our time.*

Performance Criticism in the Family of Biblical Interpretation

The "performance critic" is the grandchild of the historical critic of the Bible. Historical criticism helps to clarify one's experience of reading a biblical text by opening up the periods of time when the traditions that were set down as "scripture" were transmitted.

Interests in the processes of composition and preservation of scriptural materials, and the motivations of those who compiled and constructed them, gave birth to an interest in the *finished* texts that we now have as scripture. One difficulty with this approach is that it sets the action and experiences related by the text "back then" in some distant past, turning the text into an artifact. Interpreters have the burden of bringing the text into the present by explaining what relevance the text has and what claims it makes upon a listener. With the gradual erosion of biblical authority and the rise of biblical illiteracy, the task of interpretation through historical criticism has become even more difficult. Walter Wink points to another difficulty with historical criticism, namely that it depends upon the "detached neutrality" of the interpreter to yield valid insights. This sort of "detachment," says Wink, is no detachment at all. Rather it is a decision not to respond[5] with all our faculties—emotional, sensory, and intellectual.

"Detached" or "disinterested" silent readings of biblical texts have colored the way we have read the texts aloud to each other in Bible study or worship. Scriptures are usually presented without any of the liveliness and conviction we associate with communicating things of importance. Or, if they are presented with high energy and animation, the reader often does not demonstrate an understanding of what it *says*. The conventions and practices of oral reading that served congregations in previous eras of communication are not compelling to a generation of listeners who now expect modulated voices, energized bodies, and convincing presentations. Relationship, experience, presence, spirit, energy, embodiment, and enactment form the cluster of what is valued in communication in our media-savvy environment.[6]

One theological assumption lying behind "detached" readings is that the texts are somehow "holy" and do not require expressive speech to be understood. While I respect restraint in the communication of a text, I do want to claim that *poor* communication is no way to *revere* a text, particularly when our hope is to invoke the presence of the Holy Spirit in the *act* of communication. "Disinterested" readings lead to, well, disinterest! They imply a lack of the communicative values I describe above, namely a *lack of relationship* between a public reader and the text he or she is charged with reading. "Disinterested" or nonexpressive readings may be motivated by a sincere desire to honor a text as "holy writ." However, the *effect* of such an approach is that it places the text *out of the listeners' reach and therefore further undermines biblical authority.* With the text safely situated in a remote, irrelevant, and idealized past, the expert interpreters must explain to me *why I should care.* Why should I care about what is being communicated if the public reader performs as if he or she does not? I understand the public reading or recitation of a text to be incarnational, an embodied expression of how a text affects the reader, and a demonstration of the level of that reader's knowledge and experience of that text. Good oral communication, in the spirit of humility, is a way to recover a text's resonance and its artistry, better enabling it to make its claims upon a listener. Good communication of a text reflects the authenticity of the encounter between the Spirit of God, the reader of the text, and the listener. "Authenticity" arises out of an experiential knowledge of the text that draws upon head, heart, and gut. An authentic reading is not "detached"; it is "invested"; that is, it reveals the degree of emotional and intellectual investment that the reader has in the act of communication.

The performance critic is the child of the literary critic. Literary critics recover the resonance and affect of a text by looking at its aesthetic as well as its theological value. While appreciating *how, why,* and *where* such texts arrived in their finished form, a literary critic wonders how the texts *work* as they are in their current form and how a contemporary reader makes sense of them. Narrative criticism is the branch in the family of biblical scholarship that looks at "story" as a unit of narrative. Asking questions such as, "How is this story put together? What is its plot? Where are the conflicts, and how are they resolved? Who are the characters? What meanings are disclosed through the actions of the characters and the perspectives articulated by the narrator?" the narrative critic of scripture reads a text to determine how it functions as *literature as well as theology.* "Form," says the narrative critic, "doesn't just convey embedded meanings. Form is integral to meaning. The fact that a text is set down in narrative form instead of some other is not just a clever communicative turn. It conveys something important about the author's belief."

The narrative critic helps the reader to construct a *world* into which the reader enters and from which the reader returns with an expanded knowledge, not only of a text, but of the reader's own perceptions, sense of self, community, and the world the reader inhabits. Stories *transform* a reader's perception of his or her own world through the act of interpretive reading; they incite interest in the subjects and situations depicted in the stories themselves and encourage identification between the world of the story and the world of the reader.

Performance criticism is indebted to this family legacy of biblical and literary interpretive theory. Yet its other lineage is within the discipline of communication studies. "A text," says the performance critic, "is an act of communication between an author and a reader through which messages are passed." Not only is a text a *record* of communicative actions *back then.* A text also communicates *right now,* especially when transformed into living human speech through performed interpretations. Texts are open-ended to the future. As long as there are readers, a text will bear the capacity to communicate within an interpretive field that has infinite possibilities. Texts are put together in ways that affect readers in different ways. The narrative critic asks: "How is this text put together, and what is its impact?" Performance critics build upon and expand these tenets of *rhetorical* criticism. "Rhetoric uses symbols to produce effects"[7]—when one looks for the "rhetorical" elements of a text, one is looking at how speech and language *function* in the interpretation of meaning.

So what is distinctive about the performance critic? What does she do that other critics do not? What contribution does her practice make in enlarging our understanding of scripture? First, like the rhetorical critic, the performance critic is interested in how the speech and language of a text works. Second, like the literary or narrative critic, the performance critic is interested in the text itself and how it is put together. Conjoined with narrative criticism, performance of a text helps overcome "pericopitis" by helping us see a particular text as a whole piece of cloth. It helps overcome the aesthetic distance between a student of the text and the text itself by creating through performance a sense of the text's world. Through the experience of the text as sounded human speech, more dimensions of meaning are present, increasing a hearer's ability to identify with the characters, scenes, voices, and perspectives from a world of perception far removed from the reader's own experience.

Performance Criticism and the Presence of an Author

The performance critic sees the acts of reading and interpretation differently than either the narrative or rhetorical critic. By stepping into the shoes of the text's author, the performance critic steps into the auditory space between text, reader, and listener and tries to understand the perspectives, attitudes, convictions, and sensibilities of that author to communicate them to an audience. In doing these, the performance critic is not looking finally for *authorial intent.* Patrick Keifert names those critics who search behind texts for the consciousness of authors and their communities' "mind readers."[8] It is often hard to understand the intentions of one with whom we *are* intimate. How then can we know what someone whose historical identity we do *not* know (such as "Mark") *intended* for something as richly nuanced as a gospel? Performance critics do spend time behind texts to learn what they can about their contexts and traditions of interpretation. But they do not assume that a magic key to meaning lies there. Performance critics, like any responsible critic of scripture, look not for "keys" but for correctives when looking down the long, twisting, and shadowy paths toward the text's origins.

The performance critic is after neither the identity nor intentions of the author, but an impression of the authorial *presence* that marks a text and its affect. A performance critic does not aim in the manner of an actor to "impersonate" the character of "Mark" to speak his words. We do not embark on a search for an "historical" Mark. Should the performer want to do a "one-person show" on the author of Mark's gospel, he or she would have nothing to go on except the text itself. The performance critic is concerned rather with the *implied author* of Mark's gospel, that is, the "persona the interpreter creates to bring a consistent meaning to the entire text."[9] To perform, or *carry this authorial interpretation to completion,* the performance critic "takes the risk of reproducing the self created by the writer in the text for an audience."[10]

How does the listener experience the "self created by the writer" in the text in performance? The listener experiences the performer not as "Mark" but as the *embodied presence* of the *implied author* of the gospel. What listeners experience in performance is the effect of an author's language, an effect that is embodied through a performer's speech and gesture. To understand the nature of language, one must take into account how language *performs*, that is, what it does, particularly what it does in the space between the performer and the audience. A performance of language is contextual and subject to norms, values, rules, and conventions that shape the discourse and how it is received. The performance critic interprets a text by embodying the "literary self" of the one who is telling the story, writing the letter, singing a psalm, or offering an apocalyptic vision. The cognitive and emotional affect of a text is what leads the performer into the world of the text. Effect is checked by knowledge of a text in its various contexts of interpretation. Through performed interpretation, both performer and listener are faced with the embodied presence of the author, whose impression is left upon the text.

Performance and the Transmission of Tradition

Another literal meaning of the word *performance* is "form coming through," a dynamic process whereby language fixed in print is *transformed* into living, human speech. In the case of the gospel of Mark, for example, we have a literary form that we identify as a "gospel." "Gospel" is a blurred genre, a collage holding together in creative tension elements of biography, history, miracle story, oral interpretation, preaching, and even tragedy. In our conventional practice we read short bits of a gospel shortly before the sermon that comments on it. Consequently, we have lost a sense of the whole! This is likely not the way our early ancestors in the faith experienced these texts. What we now call "Christian scripture" bore some kind of relationship to the dynamic oral traditions and performance conventions that began to swirl around the memory of Jesus and the experience of the Risen Lord by his early disciples and the churches they formed. The literature that this early movement produced bore the residue of those traditions and distant memories of their "coming through" in performance. In fact, the *form* of these texts was indistinguishable from its *performance*; interpretation was an enactment of attitudes, experiences, and convictions conveyed in the gospels.

Until recently, what has been missing in biblical scholarship is a consideration of the relationships between the performers of those traditions, the performances, and their audiences. Performers were the primary interpreters of those traditions; performance was the way the earliest auditors first experienced what we now have as the *New* Testament. The discipline of biblical studies is taking a performance turn, that is, toward the understanding of the centrality of the performer in the dynamic processes of composition, preservation, and transmission of texts that over time and use became sacred to the Christian Church.

Performance as a Strategy of Reading

Here a great divide opens that separates the contemporary readers of Mark from their ancestors in the ancient Greco-Roman culture that surrounded the text. The Bible exists for us in book form. "Reading" the Bible is done in solitary silence in the quiet of one's own "personal" space. There are, of course, group readings in Bible studies, worship services, and classes. We assume, however, that anyone may possess a Bible, silently decode inscribed marks on a page, and have access to its meaning. Authoritative interpreters understand how to employ the varied disciplines of biblical criticism to open fields of meaning. Readers sense they are being addressed by these texts, especially if they are reading with the eyes of faith. Performance criticism challenges and complements these notions of reading and study by placing *performed interpretation in community*—not the silent, solitary reader—at the center of our concern.

I began to research and practice performance criticism when I first felt addressed in a startling way by a biblical text in performance. The setting was a reception in the home of one of my professors, Dr. Robert Jewett. The season of Advent was upon us. Biblical scholars from all over the world were in Chicago attending the annual meeting of the Society of Biblical Literature, and Dr. Jewett had invited some of his closest colleagues to his get-together. At one point in the evening, our host asked Dr. Thomas Boomershine to "tell us a Christmas story." With calm and composure, Tom began: "And it happened in those days that a decree went out from Caesar Augustus, that the entire world should be enrolled..." It was Luke's gospel story of Jesus' birth. It was a story I had been hearing all my life! It was a text taken from a body of literature to which the men and women in this room had devoted their entire careers! And yet, *in performance* that story had an immediacy and vitality that—in my experience—it had lost through countless public and private readings. A performed interpretation made the "familiar *unfamiliar*" and released the story to speak in a new way. As I looked around that room, I noted I was not the only one who felt addressed by that text. A room full of eminent biblical scholars seemed to be hearing it for the first time. Why? Because Tom had presented an interpretation that attended not only to the dynamics of oral communication but also to those influences that brought the text to us. By means of sound, attitude, gesture, and intention Tom had subverted ingrained habits of reading and interpretation (even presentation!) and given the familiar text a new hearing.

The Performer of the Text as "Maestro"

Boomershine's performance claimed that the text was "scripture" and also had value as a story. It was not simply some entertaining

story that might be told during Christmastide. By presenting the
text as the scripture of the church in performance, Tom dramatized
his own Christian belief that biblical texts make claims on believers
that other texts do not. And yet the claim a text of scripture makes
upon its listener does not arise only from the text itself. The claim
also arises from the authority conferred upon it through its use in
the common life and practice of the church. It is difficult to imagine
"use" of a text without having some concept of the text *performed*
in the life of the church. To understand what the claim of scripture
might be, we must engage in interpretation. To more fully grasp
how the text speaks to the church, we need to take *performed*
interpretations into account.

As he stood there in the company of those scholars, it was easy
to imagine Boomershine as a "maestro" in front of an orchestra.
Patrick Keifert draws the analogy between "the interpreter of a biblical
text and a chamber orchestra playing a Mozart symphony."[11]
Imagine the company of scholars in that room as a company of
interpreters who have acquired and practiced a blend of intuition,
knowledge, and technical skill to lead students of scripture to
faithful enactments and performed interpretations. Now imagine
Boomershine stepping out from among them like the Greek actor
from the chorus to speak the words of a text they all know and
recognize. Though each one has his or her own informed
interpretation of that text, Boomershine becomes in that instant
the primary interpreter of that text. To arrive at this moment, the
performer draws upon a lifetime of prayer, study, and attention to
enactment. The fruit? A rendition of a text that is faithful, evocative,
and deeply compelling. The act reminds them all of how crucial
the performance of the virtuoso is for the ongoing life of the text
within the community of saints and scholars alike. The church
needs to call out "maestros" who will develop the competencies
needed for doing performed interpretations of its scriptures.

The Community of Faith as "Performers" of the Text

The church also needs to become more intentional in performing scripture in everyday life! As valuable as the virtuoso is for our
understanding of scripture, the primary task of *performing scripture*
lies with the community of faith. The Christian community is not
at a loss for "maestros" of biblical interpretation, even if only a few
do performed interpretations. Interpreting scripture is a lively
enterprise, at least among a class of highly trained scholars. The
task of interpretation is left to either an elite group of scholars or

professional preachers whose creative and imaginative work with texts intimidate those who sit in pews without the time or training. Now here it seems I am issuing a call for yet another subgroup within the elite—those whose performed interpretations seek visibility in the professional guilds and societies, thus further removing the enterprise of biblical interpretation from the church. Even though performance criticism seeks to enliven the church's engagement with its scripture through lively speech, embodied gesture, and thoughtful study, the danger is that a new class of "specialists" who offer performed interpretations of texts will deepen the church's alienation from its scripture. What is needed is a model of performance that not only honors the skill and efficacy of a solo interpreter but also a concept of the community of faith as the primary performers of scripture. The primary "site" for the performance of scripture is not the stage or chancel, or even the space of the church. The "site" for the performance of "Holy Scripture" is within the sphere of everyday life that Christians live. When the story of Jesus and the earliest Christian communities "comes through" the organization, life, activity, and liturgical practice of the community founded in Jesus' name, then the gospel is performed in its most complete sense.[12] The solo performer of a selection from scripture becomes the model for the church as it struggles to perform its scripture in the world it serves. As the performer uses the resources of his or her study, memory, and bodily expression in the classroom or chancel, so also does the church use its resources and practices to make the subject of its scripture visible and knowable in the world.

Performing the "Ending" of Mark's Gospel

One of the most vexing texts in all of the New Testament brings home this point about the community being the primary site for the performance of "gospel." Do you recall how the gospel of Mark ends? Three pious women with designs on anointing the body of the crucified Jesus in accordance with their burial customs anxiously approach the tomb. So focused are they on their task, they have forgotten about the large stone that has been rolled across the entrance. When they arrive, they are startled to find that the stone has already been rolled away! Upon closer investigation inside the tomb, they find a "young man, dressed in a white robe, sitting on the right side" (16:5).

So far we have the makings of a fine story! It has suspense, shock, and conflict. A performed interpretation would aim to restore the effect of these narrative elements, elements that have been flattened from overuse and inexpressive reading. Take the time to prepare for a performed interpretation to experience this text as if for the first time and you will see. Become familiar enough with the structure, language, and imagery of the text to speak the words as if they are your own. *Then let yourself experience the difficulty of speaking Mark's perplexing ending. How does one speak 16:8?*[13]

When Mark leaves us with *"gar"* (a Greek preposition) at the end of verse 8, Mark frustrates the desire for a formal ending that we bring with us to the narrative. A literal translation—"They said nothing to anyone, they were afraid for…"—leaves us hanging. Later scribes were also uncomfortable with this ending. Matthew and Luke, who probably used Mark's text to construct their own, offer us appearance stories and a fuller account of what took place following the dramatic announcement of Jesus' resurrection. Some unnamed scribe or scribes even added verses 9–20 to Mark's own gospel to harmonize it with the other three.

A performance critic with knowledge of the conventions that surround this text would recognize that the ending is an "ellipse," a frequent occurrence in the literature of the day. One trained either in rhetoric or the performance of literature in that time would have interpreted the ellipse as "gesture here." *In other words, the "ending" of Mark's gospel is not a word but a gesture!*[14] A "gesture" was broadly defined in the writing about performance in Mark's day. It could be a facial expression, the posture or position of the body, or movement of the hands. On occasions when I have performed this text, I have raised both my hands, lifted my shoulders slightly, cocked my head slightly to the left and have tried to convey with my facial expression an attitude that reads (I hope): *What happens next is up to us.*

No performer can control the response to the text anymore than the implied author of Mark's gospel could. As I have said, the early Christians would not have experienced this gospel except as it was performed! And no performance will be the same as another. Still, one thing becomes clearer to me about the gospel of Mark as I perform it: The "action" of Mark's gospel is performed—that is, "carried through to completion"—in the *actions of the community* to which it is given. And what is that "action" of that gospel? First, the realm of God broke into the world in the wake of the ministries of Jesus of Nazareth and John the baptizer. Second, the realm of God breaks in through the faithful performance of the gospel by communities of faith. Finally, faithful performance of the gospel has the power to turn the world, as it is known by those communities, upside down and inside out. The complication of the action of Mark's gospel is this: The abiding presence of Jesus breaks the grip of evil but confounds even his most cherished intimates while evoking confession and faith from unexpected voices in unexpected places.

Doesn't this "action" play itself out in our faith communities? And how does that action end? It ends as this gospel does—with followers like us who are perplexed and bewildered at the good news of Jesus' resurrection, who say nothing to anyone about it because of fear, and who do not know where to look for him.

Faithful performance of Mark's gospel has two polarities. At one end stands the individual who seeks to offer a performed interpretation of the words, actions, and effect of the text of Mark as it is given. If that performer accepts Mark's gospel as scripture, then the struggle to internalize and speak the text becomes emblematic of the performer's struggle to understand what the text is *doing* in the performer's experience of Christian discipleship. At the other end lives a community marked by the claim made upon it by an enigmatic and unsettling "Son of God." A "way" has been prepared for the community to walk, and its path promises to be a difficult one. Along that way, the community will continue to be perplexed and divided, impatient and self-serving. Power structures will be exposed and confronted, and there will be consequences. Yet, the action the community performs is surrounded by divine promise—the realm of God *has* broken in and out in front, making the way for us: "[Y]ou will see him, just as he told you" (Mk. 16:7b).

PART TWO

Sermons from Mark

8

Believe the Good News

Mark 1:15

MARK LOVE

Compositional Comments

I have preached from this text before. On those occasions I focused on developing the theological vocabulary found in Jesus' announcement: eschatology, kingdom of God, repentance, believing. I used the text primarily as a springboard for tracing theological trajectories. Surely, this is a legitimate use of a text for preaching. Still, it was interesting to begin this sermon with Morna Hooker's notions of beginnings and endings. The initial burden of reading for this sermon was making sense of the overall narrative, not the relative importance of certain theological notions. Hooker's insightful reading of Mark, particularly how the beginning and ending of the gospel work together to leave an overall impression of the story, caused me to focus on aspects of this text that otherwise might only appear as window dressing or even needless detail. In particular, my attention focused on the way Galilee functions throughout the story. The short ending of Mark (16:1–8), which I take to be the original, is in many ways an invitation for the story to continue. The angel invites Jesus' followers, particularly Peter, to join the resurrected Lord where the story began in Mark 1:14—Galilee.

As readers of this story, we are invited to join the disciples in meeting the resurrected Jesus again in Galilee, moving deeper into the story of one who expresses the kingdom of God in selfless service, even to the point of death on a cross. Here, in attention to beginning and ending, lay Craddock's insistence that listeners be enlisted as participants in the sermon. How could I drop them into this story in ways that were vivid and close? This required serious imaginative effort. We live a long way from the meanings attached to Galilee in Mark's world. How could the sermon help us to participate in this reality? For better or worse, I chose the metaphor of a political campaign to locate the respective values of Jerusalem and Galilee. Mark has located this good news about the nearness of the kingdom of God in an unlikely candidate from an unlikely region, a candidate not likely to do well in the rough and tumble realities of Jerusalem.

Yet, it is precisely the unlikely nature of the story that allows it to be more than just business-as-usual. Here, the social location of Galilee provides just the right backdrop for an against-the-grain kingdom. Theology comes not just from the vocabulary or the word studies, but also from paying attention to rhetoric and social location. Hopefully, the sermon awakens listeners to the real possibility of denying the humble origins of our story, which is a denial of Jesus himself. Equally important, the sermon hopes to point to the hopeful possibility that Jesus is always willing to begin again with us if we will meet him in Galilee.

The Sermon: Believe the Good News

Now after John was arrested, Jesus came to Galilee, proclaiming the good news of God, and saying, "The time is fulfilled, and the kingdom of God has come near; repent, and believe in the good news." (Mark 1:14–15)

Good News about God

Mark has news for us today. More than that, the evangelist has *good* news for us. Better than that, it's good news about God. And we could stand a little of that today. After all, plenty of bad news is attached to God's name these days. We are always hearing about suicide bombers, jihadists, "Christian" militias in Sudan, all using "In God We Trust" as a justification for violence. Or, we hear televangelists telling us that the hurricanes on the Gulf Coast are God's punishment for the sins of New Orleans. God, it seems, is destroying cities. Plenty of bad news about God these days. Maybe God could use a better press agent.

He's got one in Mark. These verses near the front of Mark's gospel come as a welcome press release concerning God. Good news! The time is fulfilled. Change is in the air. Business as usual is no longer the only game in town. The kingdom of God has come near. Regime change is afoot, making it possible to call someone other than Caesar, "Lord." A new ordering of the world—the way God would order things—is coming into view. Jesus, in the fullness of time, has come to show us what life looks like when God is calling the shots. Amid all the bad news about God floating around these days, Mark wants us to know that when you see God through the story of Jesus, you've got good news.

The Trouble with a Galilean Candidate

Now, I'm sure Mark knows his stuff here, inspired author and all. But if I had written these verses, I might have left off the stuff about John the Baptist being in Herod's prison. Let's stay on message here. We're announcing good news. Let's keep the message upbeat. The kingdom of God has come near. Let's leave the bit about this wild-eyed cousin of Jesus being in prison for others to find out, distance ourselves a bit from this nagging detail. Later we can say, "Of course, Jesus supports John as he would any family member. We really have nothing else to say until this matter runs its course." Then back to our message. "The kingdom of God has come near." While we're critiquing this news release, I'd downplay this business about Galilee. Do we really want to announce this thing as a Galilean movement? Again, I'm sure Mark knows what he's doing here, but why not announce the coming of the kingdom in Jerusalem, maybe in Solomon's portico, the temple lit just to make the press pictures dramatic? We want them to say, "David's son in David's city: Your Messiah."

I probably just don't understand how all of this works. Maybe starting in Galilee is a little like having the first primaries in Iowa and New Hampshire. Start small, test your message with certain voter types. Raise money off of a good showing. But make sure you have Super Tuesday in your sights and that you have a good organization in Texas and California and New York and Michigan and Florida, the big delegate states. When you get to the convention at Madison Square Garden or the Fleet Center or…the temple in Jerusalem, you enter triumphantly with balloons and placards and signs and a Fleetwood Mac song. You arrive having all your endorsements lined up and the name of the one who will join you on the ticket and maybe even a few names of potential cabinet members. (James and John have a few suggestions here.) Make no mistake about it! By the time you get to the big city, you want to be hailed as the winner, the next great leader. Jerusalem is where the story ends in triumph, where you get a ten-point bump in the polls and catapult beyond your competition.

Not everyone can get from Galilee to Jerusalem. We know the names of those who don't get all the way to the convention. Howard Dean, Steve Forbes, to name a couple. Like these candidates, Galileans are notoriously hot starters but poor finishers. It's not that Galilee doesn't produce leaders. It's that Galilee produces nutcases. Wild-eyed prophets who have little savvy with regard to the ways of survival in an empire wary of insurgencies. It's one thing to get a crowd in the wilderness among disaffected peasants looking for anyone spouting hope about a kingdom of God. It's still another thing to take this show to Jerusalem and translate hope into power where it really matters.

Again, I don't want to tell Mark how to get Jesus triumphantly to Jerusalem, but with a start like this I can just imagine what the pundits, the experts on would-be messiahs, will be saying. I can hear them on the late night news shows. "Look, Ted, undoubtedly this guy has a certain appeal. We all like talk about the kingdom of God. Who, after all, likes Roman rule? This stuff plays great with the crowds. But he can't win. He'll just be a footnote when all is said and done. These guys are real dangerous. I mean, let's be serious. He's no better than many Gentiles. Look at whom he eats with and how he treats the Sabbath. I can't imagine him doing well in Jerusalem. And let's hope that's the case, because these acts of his are more than just amusing sideshows." The hatchet guys will be out on the trail whispering rumors. Can you hear them? "Why does this fellow speak this way? It's blasphemy!" "Why," they ask with an arched eyebrow, "does he eat with tax collectors and sinners?" "Why do his disciples break the law on the Sabbath?" "He has Beelzebul, and by the ruler of demons he casts out demons." And behind the scenes, they'll work to make sure he can't win. They'll plot to destroy him. I'm sure that Mark can get him safely to Jerusalem, but as a follower I've got to question what kind of start we're off to here. And, confidentially, I'm not the only one. It seems Peter has some issues about how this campaign is being run.

Aren't You One of the Galileans?

Peter had long since left his nets on the shores of the Sea of Galilee behind—and anything else that mattered to him—when the rooster crowed. Who can blame a guy for getting a little starry-eyed? Peter hitched his wagon to a rising star. We've all done it.

We've all jumped on bandwagons only to scrape an ill-fated bumper sticker off of our car when our guy proves to be another flash in the pan. But Jesus seemed like the real deal. He followed the appearance of the Elijah-esque John the Baptist. The demons submitted to him. He taught with authority, and he healed the sick. Surely, the kingdom of God has come near.

So, when Jesus asked Peter and the others what they believed about him, Peter blurted it out, "You are the Messiah!" This exclamation is filled with so much hope and expectation. We're going to Jerusalem. We've left our pathetic little lives in Galilee behind, and we're turning the world upside down. By the time the rooster crows, however, things have gone south. It's not so hard to feel badly for Peter. He has an unwilling candidate. Jesus will go to Jerusalem, but he's going to die and to die shamefully. Peter's little heart-to-heart with Jesus goes poorly—"Get behind me, Satan," Jesus tells Peter. Jesus will stay on message regardless of how it sells. The kingdom of God doesn't yield for anyone's expectations.

But worse for Peter is the scene toward the end of the gospel. Just hours before his betrayal and arrest, Jesus predicts that those closest to him will desert him. Peter boasts, "Even though all become deserters, I will not" (14:29). But Jesus assures Peter that that very night, before the rooster crows, Peter will deny Jesus. So, during Jesus' trial, when the servant-girl approaches Peter near the fire in the adjacent courtyard, we cringe and hide our eyes. "You're one of them," she says.

"I am not," Peter denies.

To those gathered around, she says it plainly, "You are one of them, for you are a Galilean." This brings Peter's instant denial and a good bit of cursing. And the rooster crowed. The promising adventure seems to have come to an end for Peter.

Better than Peter?

"Repent and believe in the good news!" This is Jesus' appeal as he announces the fullness of time and nearness of the kingdom of God. A new ordering requires new life directions. You can't have regime change without life change. "Repent," Jesus urges us. But more, he calls us to *believe* in the good news, which sometimes is easier said than done. Sometimes it is hard to believe that this story represents the nearness of the kingdom of God. After all, John the Baptist is in Herod's prison. How can this be the work of God's kingdom? Sometimes it is hard to believe that big things come from mustard seeds, that God's work can pass through a humiliated Galilean peasant, that God's kingdom is bigger than hurricanes or terrorists or massive militaries, or even 401k's and SUV's. Sometimes, it is hard to believe the good news about God.

As we have seen, it was hard for Peter. But there's good news for Peter today, and perhaps for us as well. Jesus always invites us to start again with him in Galilee. Even as Jesus predicts Peter's betrayal, he offers him hope. Jesus will be handed over to the powers that be. He will die a shameful death on a Roman cross. The powers that be will still seem like the powers that be. But Jesus promises a resurrection. The story will resume. After the resurrection, Jesus tells his followers at the Passover meal, he will meet them in Galilee. In case they forgot, the angel at the empty tomb tells the bewildered women, "Go, tell his disciples and Peter that he is going ahead of you to Galilee; there you will see him just as he told you" (16:7). The story, for Peter and for us, can always begin again—in Galilee. If we meet him, we will have the chance to remember that the coming of the kingdom always favors places like Galilee. The kingdom's natural habitat is always among the poor and overlooked and dispossessed; the proper backdrop for understanding Jesus is not halls of power or centers of influence. No, the movement of God is always most clearly seen against a humble backdrop.

By returning to Galilee, we'll have the chance to trace the story again. In doing so we can remember that God's response to worldly forms of power and violence is not more of the same. The same power that casts out demons and heals the sick is used to lay one's life down for others, or to choose to be the least, or to be the servant of all. We have the chance to believe again that this upside-down world of Jesus is the nearness of the kingdom of God. We'd like to believe that we'd fare better than did Peter the first time through the story—that we wouldn't need a return engagement in Galilee. But I have my doubts. I know I feel more comfortable in Jerusalem than in Galilee, and I think you probably do, too.

I was in a meeting a few weeks ago. We were talking about changing the date on an event at the Christian university I work for. Someone remarked that this change in date might conflict a little with the West Texas Fair and Rodeo. Someone else said over their starched white shirt that he'd been to the West Texas Fair and Rodeo, he'd seen what kind of folks attend the fair, and he doubted seriously there was any overlap in audience. A little laughter. But what about competition for motel rooms? "I don't think they stay in the same motels we do either," he replied, smiling through his perfect dental work. A round of laughter from the room. A little fun at the expense of the Galileans. What's the harm? There are no roosters in the room.

We like it in Jerusalem, and we'll have no slave girls or carnival barkers reminding us that we're Galileans. If we will, we have the chance today to begin again with Jesus precisely so that we might remember that the gospel is not just another version of the "good life." The gospel is not just so much grease on the skids for a life of smooth sailing. For heaven's sake, John the Baptist is in Herod's prison. This is an against-the-grain story. This is regime change, life beyond business as usual, not a way for us to pursue our current course more efficiently. A new ordering has appeared that will require changed allegiances from us all and the courage to believe that this indeed qualifies as good news.

Maybe you're tired of hearing preachers critiquing our way of life. I'm a little tired of saying it myself. But we better be clear about it or make sure no roosters are around to crow in board rooms or car dealerships or at the prayer breakfast in Washington when you deny you're a Galilean. Let's hope for no roosters when you let the slave girl near the fire know you're only committed to some parts of the Jesus story. There's no good news there.

The Kingdom of God Has Come Near

The images of those who suffered in hurricanes Katrina and Rita were overwhelming. Their impact on me was greater than the similarly devastating pictures in the aftermath of the tsunami in 2004. This impact is due to more than proximity, though this is surely part of it. No, this disaster has brought the homeless poor of a U.S. city out of the shadows and into our communities as evacuees. They are sleeping in the Wal-Mart down the street. Our campus announcements have to do with the needs of real life people displaced through these disasters. Some are here with us today in worship. I wonder, in light of our text today, I wonder if the presence of these "refugees" among us is a summons to Galilee. I wonder if this isn't the voice of the resurrected Jesus calling, "The time is fulfilled. The kingdom of God has come near. Leave life as you know it. Be done with business as usual, and join me in Galilee to give your lives for these people." Does that sound like good news to you?

It does to me, because it sounds like Jesus. It sounds like casting out demons and healing the sick. It sounds like forgiving sins and acting in power—God's power. It sounds like the first becoming last and the last becoming first. And it sounds like a welcome respite from the constant grind of accomplishing, competing, building, growing, and ruling that seems to offer us way less than it promises.

"Now after John was arrested, Jesus came to Galilee, proclaiming the good news of God,...'Repent, and believe in the good news.'"

9

A Window into the Kingdom

Mark 2:13–17

MARK FROST

Compositional Comments

This sermon is based on Fred Aquino's insights into incarnation theology from the book of Mark. Aquino states that God is in the business of rearranging relationships, reconstructing social constructs, and renegotiating boundaries. He points out that the logic of God's kingdom is that the people we least expect are invited to the table with us. He also observes that in Mark the people least expected to understand the message are the ones who do, while those one would expect to "get it" are the ones who do not.

In the sermon I attempt first to portray as vividly as possible the way in which Jesus boldly violated social boundaries by eating at Levi's table. Then, I move slowly—and stealthily—toward the conclusion that, in the face of similar social boundaries, it is we in the church who often don't "get it." In the sermon, I incorporate a couple of insights from Fred Craddock. One is the admonition to let Mark speak on his own terms, without interpreting his story through the other gospels. Accordingly, my description of the nature of the kingdom of God is drawn exclusively from imagery recorded in Mark. The only other biblical passage I cite is from Isaiah, a book Mark himself makes use of in his opening chapter. I also try to use Craddock's suggestion to add immediacy to the sermon by telling the story in the present tense.

Finally, I incorporate Morna Hooker's insights about the importance of Mark's beginning and ending for understanding the message of the book. After telling the story of Jesus at Levi's house, I refer back to the beginning of the gospel to place the event in the context of an announcement of the kingdom of God. Later, I refer to Mark's unfinished ending as a way of moving the audience toward possible applications of the message to their own experience.

The Sermon: A Window into the Kingdom

Advertising guru Roy H. Williams says, "Every door of opportunity begins as a window in your mind. Look through that window of imagination and glimpse a world that could be, someday. Keep looking…Be patient…And watch it grow into a door of opportunity through which you might pass into an entirely different future."[1]

I want to show you such a window today. I'll do my best to pull the curtains, open the blinds, and wipe away the smudges so you can get a good look at a fascinating world on the other side. What you do then will be up to you. Will you be enthralled enough to keep looking through the window, or will you turn away too soon and forget what you see? Will you allow the image of the other world to form completely in your mind? Will you be patient enough to keep looking until a door of opportunity opens before you? And when it does, will you have the courage to walk through that door?

The window is found in the second chapter of Mark's gospel:

Jesus went out again beside the sea; the whole crowd gathered around him, and he taught them. As he was walking along, he saw Levi son of Alphaeus sitting at the tax booth, and he said to him, "Follow me." And he got up and followed him.

And as he sat at dinner in Levi's house, many tax collectors and sinners were also sitting with Jesus and his disciples—for there were many who followed him. When the scribes of the Pharisees saw that he was eating with sinners and tax collectors, they said to his disciples, "Why does he eat with tax collectors and sinners?" When Jesus heard this, he said to them, "Those who are well have no need of a physician, but those who are sick; I have come to call not the righteous but sinners." (2:13–17)

At first glance, we almost certainly will misunderstand this scene. Twenty-one centuries of history have so fogged our window that we see only the vague outlines of the story, missing crucial details. We see Jesus walking by the sea and calling a disciple. The words are identical to the call of the fishermen—Simon, Andrew, James, and John—in the opening chapter. And Levi's response is identical to theirs. He leaves his profession and becomes a follower of the teacher. That strikes us as curious and may cause us to marvel at the power of the personality that elicits such an immediate response. But on the other side of the window, the first-century-in-Palestine side, the observers of the scene are mortified. What has so possessed the teacher that he deems a stinking tax collector fit to follow him? You see, these people know some things we do not. They understand that tax collectors are their own countrymen, chosen by the Roman occupiers more for their ability to maximize revenues than for their integrity. They know that when a Jew makes the fateful decision to enter the revenue service, he is excommunicated from the synagogue as a heretic and a traitor. They understand that a tax collector, like any other disreputable person, is not allowed to be a witness in a court of law. They all know people who have been cheated out of their meager earnings by unscrupulous tax collectors. No one needs to explain to them why the rabbis put tax collectors in the same class as murderers and armed robbers.

Does the teacher not know this as well? Surely he does, which can only mean he doesn't care. Evidently he does not care about the uncleanness that will forever taint his ministry. Surely he understands that this fateful selection will stand as an obstacle to the hearing of his message for virtually everyone, from the poorest peasant to the most sophisticated scholar. It is as if the president nominated to the Supreme Court a gay white male anti-abortion pro-gun agnostic environmentalist, in the process alienating every conceivable constituency. And what's worse, Jesus *eats* with Levi and his ilk. He shares a feast with all kinds of folks who have been kicked out of the synagogue for their moral filthiness and spiritual bankruptcy. There he sits with gamblers and crooks, prostitutes and pimps, muggers and molesters. Look at him casually chatting and laughing out loud while the air around him turns blue with cigarette smoke and profanity and the alcohol flows freely. If this is the teacher's idea of proper conduct and respectful decorum, *we* may want to think twice about listening to him.

On our side of the window, twenty-first–century America, it is hard to find a parallel situation that doesn't trivialize what's happening in this scene. We may think of our distrust for IRS agents but still not understand the utter disdain directed at these first-century tax farmers. We can imagine the discomfort of dining in a dimly lit bar with a crowd of crude loudmouths, but not grasp the abject disgrace Jesus brought on himself. We can admire the kindness of a popular teen sitting at the "nerd's table" in the cafeteria, but still not understand the raw courage it took for Jesus to sit at Levi's table. However imperfectly we understand the scene, we do have something in common with the folks on the first-century side of the window. We wonder why Jesus behaves as he does. One thing is obvious. Jesus intentionally violates social norms. When you see a purple-haired teen dressed in studded black clothing, sporting dozens of gaudy tattoos and grotesque body piercings, you may not understand the message she is sending; but you can be certain she is sending it quite deliberately. Just as obviously, Jesus purposefully takes his seat at Levi's table. But what, exactly, is the message? Is it an angry backlash against a system that makes him feel worthless? Is it a protest against the dehumanizing and depersonalizing powers of the establishment? Or is it merely a post-adolescent need to call attention to himself through the most outrageous behavior imaginable?

Here's where we have the advantage over the people on the first-century side of the window. You see, this isn't our first time through the story. We've read Mark's account from beginning to end. If we have been attentive, we know some things the people beyond our window do not. Mark begins the story by identifying Jesus as the Christ, the Messiah, the very Son of God. In the opening verse, Mark tells us that this story is good news. Thirteen verses later, we discover that this good news is about the imminent approach of the kingdom of God (1:14–15). Now, knowing all of this might confuse us even further. What could the raucous revelry going on at Levi's house possibly have to do with the kingdom of God? Are we to believe that God would be present in such an unlikely setting or that he would choose to offer his good news to the baddest "bad news bears" of the world?

Having skimmed ahead in Mark's story, we're not terribly surprised. We've learned that when it comes to the kingdom of God, we should expect the unexpected. We've come to understand that the kingdom of which Jesus speaks is a strange place indeed. It is a realm in which people with 20/20 vision fail to see. Those with perfect hearing do not understand what they hear (4:11–12). It is a place where the expected formulas for success in life work in reverse. Ambition is counterproductive (4:19). Hard work is irrelevant (4:26–27). Impressive physical attributes count for nothing (4:31–32). Losers are saved, and savers lose everything (8:35–36). Those with no status or credentials receive preferential entry into the kingdom, while those with wealth, status, and power are turned away with the suggestion that they would have greater success trying to cram a camel through the eye of a needle (10:13–25). Now we begin to see more clearly through our window. At Levi's feast, Jesus isn't a guest; he is the host. This meal is designed to be a foretaste of the great Messianic feast of which the prophet Isaiah spoke long ago:

> On this mountain the LORD of hosts will make for all peoples
> a feast of rich food, a feast of well-aged wines,
>> of rich food filled with marrow, of well-aged wines
>> strained clear.
> And he will destroy on this mountain
>> the shroud that is cast over all peoples,
>> the sheet that is spread over all nations;
>> he will swallow up death forever.
> Then the Lord GOD will wipe away the tears from all faces,
>> and the disgrace of his people he will take away from all
>> the earth,
>>> for the LORD has spoken. (Isa. 25:6–8)

On this occasion, Jesus isn't just talking *about* the kingdom; he's *demonstrating* the kingdom. Through his loving presence, he's removing the shroud of disgrace that had clung to his guests for so long. He's wiping away the tears of rejection and ostracism, destroying the barriers erected by religious tradition, ethnic arrogance, and self-righteous legalism. In their place, he's laying down a different law, a principle aptly stated in John Shea's poem, *The Indiscriminate Host*: "The banquet is open to all who are willing to sit down with all."[2] Jesus is practicing a radical inclusion that offends the keepers of exclusivity. They huff and puff and demand to know how any alleged spiritual leader could justify associating with such reprobates. But the outcast and marginalized people of the world, the people who know the sting of rejection and condemnation, understand. They know that what we see through our window is truly good news. As South African Archbishop Desmond Tutu says, what he loves most about Jesus is his "wonderfully low standards."[3] Jesus defends his standards by reciting— with a playful grin, I think—his version of an old proverb: If you're looking for a doctor, go to where the sick folks are (2:17).

Now, if we were very attentive back at the beginning of Mark's story, we learned that his brief account of Jesus' life, including the scene at Levi's house, is but the *beginning* of the good news of the kingdom (1:1). If we've really understood the end of the story, we know that Mark leaves it unfinished, likely with the expectation that *we* will complete it. That means that what we see through our window is more than a fascinating period piece; it is a challenge for us to demonstrate the good news of the kingdom as clearly on our side of the window as Jesus does on his.

But how are we to do this? On my side of the window, in my insulated existence, I tend to be blind to the kinds of barriers that were so prominent in Jesus' world unless I choose to see them. In my world, racial segregation has been outlawed. Discrimination of every kind is both banned and stigmatized. The values of diversity, inclusion, and acceptance are preached from every pulpit, secular as well as sacred. From my limited vantage point, only if I imagine myself in a different place or time can I clearly see how to imitate Jesus. If I lived in India, I would invite "Untouchables" into my home. Had I lived in the Deep South in the 1950s, I would refuse to sit at the "whites only" lunch counter. If I were an Israeli, my living room would be filled with Palestinians. Oh, how simple it is to be courageous and Christ-like when one is merely an observer from a distance.

Maybe it's important for us to grasp small and seemingly insignificant opportunities to break social boundaries. For instance, when our church hosts the Christnet homeless shelter,[4] we do not make the clients stand in a cafeteria line for their food. No, we serve them at their tables as honored guests. Then we sit down and eat with them instead of isolating ourselves in the kitchen. Maybe in some tiny way this demonstrates the kingdom of God to our world. Perhaps we could periodically leave an unexpectedly oversized tip for a not-so-efficient waiter. The cost could hardly be called sacrificial, but maybe that's a way we could imitate the lavish generosity of Jesus. Maybe in our daily comings and goings, we could consciously try to be cordial toward people who have reason to expect we would not be kindly disposed toward them.

I do know that Jesus' conduct at Levi's house has led me to make a simple change in my behavior. I perform a lot of weddings for people in the community. I used to respectfully decline invitations to wedding receptions at which I knew the majority of attendees would be non-church-going, "worldly" people. I did so because I knew I would be uncomfortable in that setting. A few years ago, I made the commitment to start accepting those invitations. Now, I go to lots of wedding receptions, quietly sipping my diet cola in dingy halls that reek of cigarette smoke and cheap beer, hoping that somehow my presence will communicate the love of Jesus to the crowd of revelers.

I have to tell you, all this seems pretty tame next to the picture of Jesus. For him, real risk is involved. The broad early section of Mark in which we see Jesus at Levi's house and in which we find Jesus assailing other societal barriers ends on an ominous note. "The Pharisees went out and immediately conspired with the Herodians against him, how to destroy him"(3:6). Two groups who would never dream of sharing a common meal nevertheless agree to cooperate in eliminating a common threat. Make no mistake about it: On Jesus' side of the window, eating with the wrong crowd poses a grave threat to the social order and can get you killed! I have to tell you that I'm pretty happy to be here on my side of the window, where multiculturalism is celebrated and inclusion is universally encouraged, where I do not see the kinds of social boundaries that one crosses only at grave risk.

But it's right here in my safe cocoon that a disturbing realization breaks in. The fact that I don't see oppressive social barriers doesn't necessarily mean they don't exist. It may simply mean I am one of the people with 20/20 vision who cannot see obvious abuses. Even with perfect hearing, I may be deaf to the cries of the oppressed. I think Jesus would remind me that even in my world, power and privilege still rule with ungodly force. Money is still every bit the false god that it ever was. The greed and selfishness that use power, privilege, and wealth to demean, disenfranchise, exclude, and enslave are as prevalent as ever. I think he would say that our world needs to see a demonstration of the kingdom as desperately as his did.

Recently, the Holy Spirit used current events to open my eyes to the need for bold action in assaulting unjust social barriers. The aftermath of Hurricane Katrina revealed a truth that we've tried to ignore: not only is our country still divided by race and socioeconomic class, but that division can spell the difference between life and death. I watched televised images of poor people looting stereos and video gear from flooded stores in New Orleans and thought, "I could not imagine *ever* doing something like that." But I can easily imagine myself loading up my SUV with all the necessities of life and driving to a safe haven away from the storm without giving a second thought to those left behind: the poor, the old, the sick, and the helpless—in short, the very people Jesus calls me to serve in his name. With shame, I have to admit that my sin is at least as reprehensible as that of the looters. It causes me to ask myself an uncomfortable question: as a resident of metropolitan Detroit, who are the helpless ones to whose plight I am blithely oblivious? Will it take a Katrina-sized disaster to make me realize—too late—what I should have done to help them?

The need for courageous action still exists. No doubt you remember that in July, someone burned a cross on the front lawn of an interracial couple that lives less than three blocks from our church building. And you remember our response as a church: we all signed a letter to that couple offering our sympathy and support. In that letter, we pledged to oppose attitudes that foster racial intolerance "whenever and wherever we encounter them." What you don't know, because I was ashamed to tell you, was that two days after we sent that letter, I had a conversation with a man who lives near our church building. He made some incredibly ugly and bigoted statements about African Americans. While I know my face registered shock, I failed to explicitly voice my opposition to his attitude. I'm sure that this was a test to determine if I truly believed the letter I had signed, and my courage failed! I'm thankful that after repentance and confession, God graciously granted me a second chance with this man. We had a conversation that left him with no doubt about my convictions, and that *may* have made a dent in his prejudice. But I wonder how many times we've been faced with similar challenges and have chosen the path of silence and passivity.

And so I pray that the Holy Spirit will open our eyes as we look through the window to see Jesus at Levi's house. I pray that you will be fascinated enough to keep looking through the window, allowing the image of the world on the other side to form completely in your mind. And I pray that as you look, a door of opportunity will be opened before you. Perhaps it will be an opportunity to be an advocate for someone at work or at school who has no voice. Maybe it will be an opportunity to clearly confront attitudes of prejudice and bigotry. Maybe it will be an opportunity to leave your safe, insulated, suburban world and minister to the needs of people in Southwest Detroit. Whatever the door of opportunity that opens before you, will you walk through it courageously? Or, like the disciples leaving the tomb at the end of Mark's story, will you be scared silent? Which response you choose is important. The story we've seen unfold through our window is about the imminent arrival of the kingdom of God. How it ends is up to you.

10

"Who Is Jesus?"

Mark 4:35–41/Psalm 107:23–31

DAVID FLEER

Compositional Comments

This sermon's style attempts at several points to follow Fred Craddock's sage counsel. Craddock's conversation with Kevin and his closing word in "Jesus Deeply Grieved," both found in this volume, are the most recent reminders of the evocative power of sermonic language. The sermon depends on details from the biblical text, an essential move for audiences schooled and comfortable in the objective distance created by historical critical preaching. For this reason the sermon reveals its motives and overtly signals when it moves beyond a standard objective reading to one that enlists the congregation to find engagement and life—claiming, for instance, "This story sounds different when we sit inside the boat than it did from two miles away."

The sermon, at times, retains an oral quality that "sounds" quite appropriate in the pulpit, but awkward in print. Nevertheless, I anticipate the same effect in reading that occurred in the preaching: a kind of "you are there" quality that Craddock identifies in Mark. Above all, I've attempted to listen to Mark's preaching. Respecting his words, their repetition and allusions, the sermon asks Mark's most important question, respects its fearful context, and hints at faithful responses. The sermon's form follows Mark, from the storm to the calm seas, which, as Mark shows, create an even greater fear and articulate his essential concern, "Who is this?"

I wish to thank a former undergraduate student, Brian Faust, whose performance of the storm at sea helped inspire the sermon's imagery, and Richard Ward, Fred Craddock, Morna Hooker, and each writer in this volume who encourages the sacred task of experiencing Mark as the preacher.

The Sermon: Who Is Jesus?

Who is Jesus? On Interstate 75, north of Detroit, just past the suburbs, adjacent to the freeway, stands the Dixie Baptist Church with a super-sized portrait of Jesus, visible to passing motorists. Jesus is pictured with aquiline nose, high cheek bones, groomed brows, long lashes, blue eyes, thin lips. Jesus wears light and thin brown hair, shoulder length. He appears slender, with light-colored skin, and strikes a serene, upward, heavenly gaze. He looks to be of Scandinavian descent, as if his last name is Swenson.

Is that Jesus?

Or, is Jesus better imagined in a statement like this one: "Jesus of Nazareth was a man of illegitimate birth, benevolent heart, enthusiastic mind, who set out with pretensions of divinity, ended in believing them, and was punished capitally for sedition by being gibbeted according to Roman law." So thought our country's third president, Thomas Jefferson. More interesting than Jefferson's conclusions was Jefferson's technique. He found the "real Jesus" by "abstracting what is really his from the rubbish in which it is buried, easily distinguished by its luster from the dross of his biographers, and as separable from that as the diamond from the dung hill." Dross, rubbish, and dung hill? That seems an inappropriate description for the content of Jesus' life and insensitive to the reality of ours.

Who is Jesus? Norwegian Jesus, who looks like the image in the mind of Richard Sellman who "painted him" in 1940? Or, the Jeffersonian Jesus: a diamond extracted from the rubbish of life?

Who is Jesus? This is the very question that the gospel of Mark relentlessly and creatively pursues. In Mark's gospel people are crowding in to see. Loaves and fishes, who wouldn't? Crowds push in, jam doors, block city entrances, intrude on Jesus' private life so that he can't take a meal or get a moment's rest. But the crowd only wants a glimpse. His family thinks he's lost his marbles. Townsfolk say, "The son of Joseph? I don't believe it!" And, the people who do get up close and personal are filled with *fear*.

Who is Jesus? It's not an easy question to answer. It's not an easy story to tell. It gets complicated and nuanced, like most good stories. As a storyteller, Mark is no hyper evangelist with unfounded confidence. He is indirect and honest, wanting us to believe something about Jesus. A collector of stories, he has plucked these from some source and arranged them, like a bouquet, so that the central question of his rich array of tales is voiced by the twelve disciples the moment the storm calms, "Who is this...?"

Mark is indirect, but he is certainly well organized. Take a look at one section of Mark's work. He has brought together four stories to his portrait of Jesus. In the scene following the storm Jesus is up against a legion of demons inhabiting a man living in a cemetery, bound with chains, made mad by the devil. Jesus shows his power over evil (5:1–20). Jairus's twelve-year-old daughter is seriously ill, and then dead. Jesus raises her from the dead (5:21–24, 35–43). A woman with a hemorrhage, sick for years, is incurable. Jesus heals her (5:25–34). This is Mark's collage, a collection of stories showing Jesus' power over nature, evil, sickness, and death.

Who is Jesus? This is Mark's all-consuming question, his central interest, his main concern. However, Jesus' identity is not Mark's only issue. Mark wants to examine the response to Jesus as well.

I *apologize.* I'm being so *academic,* giving you the "literary lay of the land." I sound like a tour guide, like some professor handing out notes, leading you along the Sea of Galilee's shoreline. You have your cameras hanging around your necks, wide-brimmed hats protecting you from the sun. I stand on the shore and point out to the sea and explain, "Sudden and powerful storms have been known to funnel down the Galilean Hills and rush out to the sea. The force of the wind would cause great billows to arise."

You nod politely and ask a friend to take your picture as you stand on the shore and use the sea as background for your picture. If a storm were to break out...why, we'd pull our jackets over our heads, scamper for shelter, and worry about the rain's effect on our hair and makeup and complain, "I hope the moisture doesn't damage my new camera."

Our old Sunday school ways come back over us. Seated in our second grade wooden chairs, semicircle around the flannel graph, Sister Mortenson is our teacher. Flannelgraph Jesus in his white robe, arms under his head, on a gray fluffy pillow, at the boat's stern. Sister Mortenson places gray clouds in the corner of the board, a lightning bolt shooting down and white-capped waves next to the boat. Sister Mortenson's flannel tale should scare us, but we have heard this tale before. We know Jesus will stand up, arms outstretched, and calm the storm. Sister Mortenson will peel back the clouds to reveal a yellow sun shining in the flannel board corner.

When we grow up, we leave class, sit in a pew, and sing, "Master the tempest is raging…I perish, I perish dear master, O hasten to take control."[1] In four-part harmony the chorus strikes, "The wind and the sea will obey his will, peace be still, peace be still." Our experience with this story has been two-dimensional, flat, predictable, distant, and remote from our life—like an ocean gale…experienced behind the protection of the hotel room's storm glass window, gas-lit fire warming us. Safe and comfortable.

Perhaps if we stop talking about Jesus from *two miles away*, perhaps if we listen carefully to our real tour guide (Mark), and allow ourselves to move to places *he* wishes to lead us, then maybe something different might happen this time.

At the beginning of the storm story Mark takes the trouble to picture Jesus on the sea (4:1). In the span of one verse he mentions the word *sea* three times and *boat* once. For landlubbers the literal translation of the Greek is pretty dramatic: "He got into the boat and sat on the sea." That doesn't sound like bad Greek at all; "*sat on the sea*" sounds exactly like it feels when we step into the boat.

This boat is twenty-six by eight feet, and four feet deep. Its length is about a yard short of a first down, and maybe it could fit a dozen passengers, but they'd need to have an "S" on their T-shirt tags. Small boat. This isn't a Norwegian cruise ship. This is a large-sized rowboat, raised at one end. Not much more than a thin slice of wood between you and the sea floor. Step into this boat, one foot secure on land the other touching the craft's unsteady floor, moving; now both feet in, use your arms to steady yourself. Hold on to the side. Smell the wet cedar and fish. Listen to water lapping against the boat, all innocent enough…before we launch.

By the time our story really starts, we are in the *middle* of the sea. The wind is picking up, sea getting choppy, sky growing dark. Cumulous clouds—black and gray—moving in, thunder clouds darken the sun. Sail snaps, wind howls, air wet with the sea. Waves swell, and you hold on, knuckles white. The boat rises and falls, rises and plunges, jarring your teeth when you hit. Lightening flashes, thunder crashes, rings your head.

"Breathe in," you remind your self, "Breathe."

Your heart pounds, stops, races on again.

"God," you whisper, "God, help us."

The storm is violent now, the wind cuts, the sea opens and closes. The boat lists to your right. You feel it about to capsize. Waves crest and break over the deck. We are taking on water. You feel it sloshing at your calves. The boat rides heavy and low. Andrew and James are bailing water. Sea-experienced disciples are wide-eyed and afraid. They're yelling, but the wind screams louder. The boat creaks. A sharp explosive sound. Will we break apart? Ahhhhhh! At the back of the boat is Jesus. Asleep. Asleep! on the cushion.

This story sounds different when we sit inside the boat than it did from two miles away. This isn't dung hill or rubbish or dross. This is where we live. This is our life. We are in the boat, and a storm is boiling.

> And Jesus rebuked the wind and the waves and said to the sea, "Quiet, hush." And the wind died down and it became perfectly calm. And Jesus said to the disciples, "Why are you so timid? How is it that you have no faith?" And they became even more afraid and said to one another, "Who is this that even the wind and the sea obey him?" (4:39–41 paraphrased).

"Be muzzled, hush," Jesus said to the demons (1:25). Now he says to the sea, "Quiet, hush!" (4:39). Jesus controls evil. Jesus controls nature. "Hush," he says. And, like a broken animal, the sea whimpers and stills. And, as great as the storm was , so great is the calm. In the face of death he says, *Talitha Koum*. In the despair of sickness he says, *Go in peace, be well*. Into the eye of evil he says to the legion of demons, *Out!* But with the calm comes the most remarkable response. The disciples are even more afraid. *More afraid*? After the danger disappears? Why?

There exists an old song; the words have been preserved although we have lost the tune. An ancient poem, familiar to some of you, a song of deliverance.

> Some went down to the sea in ships,
>   doing business on the mighty waters;
> they saw the deeds of the LORD,
>   his wondrous works in the deep.
> For he commanded and raised the stormy wind,
>   which lifted up the waves of the sea…
>
> Then they cried to the LORD in their trouble,
>   and he brought them out from their distress;

he made the storm be still,
and the waves of the sea were *hushed*.

This poem isn't an eyewitness account in the *Jerusalem Times*. This tuneless "song" is not a reflective work by Bartholomew or some medieval monk. In fact, this poem predates Jesus, and was in print when Mark wrote his gospel. It was "out there" when Jesus calmed the storm at sea. This poem was in *Jesus'* Bible, Psalm 107.

Who is this that the wind and the sea obey him? The answer for anyone familiar with the Old Testament is clear. This is the Lord God Almighty, Yahweh who created the heavens and the earth. In this storm, when even the wind and sea obey him, the old Jewish hymn comes to mind. *God is in the boat.* So, what are we afraid of? Afraid of the storm...deep water...drowning? Afraid that the church will split? Afraid the marriage will crumble? Afraid of the pain? Yes! No wonder we are so "timid."

But, what are we *really* afraid of? *After* the storm the fear reemerges (4:41). The fact is, sometimes weeks and months after the national disaster or the personal crisis, belief is difficult. Why is that? What are we afraid of? Are we afraid God has lost interest in us? Like an early morning fog, disappeared? Walked off stage? Afraid he is not watching? Afraid...that he is asleep?

Did you notice the disciples asking, "Don't you care?" Is it that we are afraid to ask, for fear it is true? Are we afraid to ask the obvious question here? Why did the storm erupt in the first place? Yeah! Why the storm? Why did that happen? While we are at it, why did Jairus's daughter need to die? Why did that happen?

Why the storm?
Why death?
Why cancer?
Why loneliness?
Why pain?
Why?

Are we afraid to voice our suspicions and doubts to God in the boat? Maybe we're afraid that if Jesus is God, then we can't domesticate him. Can't put him on a leash, like a dog, and say, "Here, God." Can't treat him like a servant and give him a "to-do list" for the day. Maybe we're afraid that if Jesus is God then he is in control and that he'll act in his own good time. Maybe that is why we are afraid.

In the midst of our fear, Jesus asks, "Will you have faith?" He is not asking that we have faith in his miracles, faith in some theological view, or even in the historicity of this story. He asks us, "Will you have faith that Jesus is God?" Do we trust Jesus to be God?"

In recent years you and I have seen our share of storms. We've been in emergency rooms. We've visited funeral homes. We've sat in folding chairs under the green canopy. And, *this* church and *this* community have had some storms, too. Sudden disturbing revelations. The loss of a beloved brother or sister. You've been in the boat when it's taking on water. Slow-developing storms, the ones that take years to brew and never leave. Chronic pain, betrayal, abandonment, a child's poor health, loneliness, debilitating illness, no job. And yet, listen to the testimonies of the faithful. You remember the convicted presidential aide who has a religious awakening in prison and spends his life in ministry.

I know of a soldier blinded by a head wound who later credits his affliction for forcing him to develop other senses and "see" what few others can see. Someone here reinterprets sexual abuse suffered long ago and claims, "God didn't allow me to suffer for no reason"; talks of a "higher calling." Several years after a painful divorce, another says she would never have developed confidence in her own abilities if she'd remained in the marriage.

Tragedies, misfortunes, storms brewing. But, instead of crumbling or quitting, some have found meaning in what happened. Is that faith?

What I say next will be the strangest and most hopeful thing you will hear this morning. According to his biographer, Stephen Crane lived out events in his imagination long before he experienced them in reality. Contrary to expectations that a writer's works are based on past experiences, Crane wrote about events *before* he experienced them, making his fiction eerily predictive of what lay ahead. His only experiences with battle, as war correspondent, came years after he published his Civil War novel, *The Red Badge of Courage*. Crane wrote *Maggie*, his novel about a prostitute, long before he fell in love with a real-life madam. Life imitating art? Or is it that Stephen Crane seemed to be living his life backward, experiencing the future before it happened?[2]

We are not novelists. However, as for Crane, life for us is imagined *before* we live it. This is our view of scripture. This morning we have rehearsed a story that is waiting to happen…to you. Sometime in the near future you will step into a small boat and lift anchor for the middle of the sea. Just when you lose sight of land, a violent storm will hit with such unexpected force that you will despair of life itself. Your fear will arise from two sources: the storm and the unpredictable power of God revealed through Jesus of Nazareth. This will be a fearful experience because Jesus is not your servant. He is God Almighty. In the midst of your fear God will ask you to have faith—faith that God will answer your prayers—not according to your desires, not according to your needs, but according to his steadfast love. Christian faith is a difficult thing. Fortunately, for the story we are about to live, Mark has given us a script to read and perform. We have words to help us articulate our fears and faith.

Words like these: "Yes I believe. Help my unbelief."

Acts like these: "In fear and trembling she touched the hem of his garment, thinking, 'If I just touch his garment I'll be healed'" (5:27–28 paraphrased).

For those of us who have shown ourselves failures in previous storms, we have hope. To disciples like us, Jesus appears again on the sea; and with the winds howling and us straining at the oars, he says, "Take heart, it is I; do not be afraid" (6:50f).

That's who Jesus is.

11

What Do You Have to Do with Us, Son of the God Most High?

Mark 5:1–20

CHRIS BENJAMIN

Compositional Comments

Fred Craddock teaches us to respect our listeners, claiming listener responsibility is essential to effective preaching. This sermon respects the audience by allowing them to assume responsibility to hear the sermon. Following Craddock's instruction to preach all of the particularities of the text and not just "the stain in the bottom of the cup," I have attempted to let the complexities of this energetic story swirl in the limited space of the sermon.

According to Morna Hooker, Mark's gospel functions like a first-century drama. This is certainly the case with Mark 5:1–20. The text is part of a section of dramatic encounters that begins at 4:35 and ends at 6:6. The thematic question linking these dramas is fixated on Jesus' identity. Hooker notes that when such questions are raised, we need only think back to the introduction to interpret the answer. John the Baptist's statement from 1:7 seems to be the answer to the question: Jesus is the one who has come with power.

The function of this sermon is to call the hearers to identify with at least one of two points of view. First, the fearful Gerasenes, who are threatened by the terrific power and authority of Jesus, are presented sympathetically as those who try to contain the power of evil but ironically reject Jesus when he proves more powerful than the powers. Second, the point of view of the demoniac is presented as one who responds faithfully to the one who has restored him and is consequently set up as an example of faithful proclamation. The mixture of these views enables us to do what Frederick Aquino describes in this volume: to experience what it means to be fully human in the light of the gospel of Jesus Christ. Aquino's remarks on Mark's incarnational theology have helped me articulate the focus of the sermon: When we recognize Jesus as the Son of the Most High God, we also recognize the self that emerges in our faithful response.

Craddock's instructions on indirect discourse and listener responsibility have shaped the discourse of the sermon so that the hearer, rather than the preacher, resolves the implied question, "Who Are You?" The question that the demoniac asks Jesus, "What have you to do with me, Jesus, Son of the Most High God ?" (Mk. 5:7) seems to be a question that the Gerasenes could also ask. The sermon's dialogue allows us to identify with the Gerasenes and the demoniac so that we might also consider what Jesus has to do with us and what we will choose to do with him.

The Sermon: What Do You Have to Do with Us, Son of the God Most High?

Some of you know what the Gerasenes have been through. You know who you are. You have put up with those possessed by demons—not just the cemetery-dwelling varieties of evil! If you ever tried to help others who are dehumanized by legions of evil, then you know what the Gerasenes have been through. If you know what it is like to be disturbed by the howling agony of others tortured by evil, then you know what the Gerasenes have been through. If you have persistently attempted to bind these others with chains for their own protection and then feel frustration as they snap the chains, then you know what the Gerasenes have been through. If you have ever felt the numbing acceptance of learning to cope with the indignity of others twisted by the power of hell, then you know what the Gerasenes have been through. You know who you are.

I know what the Gerasenes have been through. I knew it when I visited my friend one more time at the emergency room. He was bound by the tubing of the IV that was pumping medicine into his veins to curb the pain of withdrawal. His wife had thrown him out again because he broke all the chains of covenant and support. I barely recognized this man now red-eyed and unshaven. He cut through the pain in his gut with each sharply exhaled breath. With what chain can we bind him that he will not break? What power is able to restore his dignity?

I know what the Gerasenes have been through. I knew it when I watched a woman in the courtroom for the custody hearing. Did she really want custody of her children, or did she want to make her husband pay? I am not sure she knew the answer. She had disturbed the peace many times with her weeping and wailing in worship. Every time she walked the aisle to repent of her sins we tried to establish boundaries for her own good, but she slipped through the bonds. She had lied, and every lie was making a horrible scar upon her character. She was so filled with spirits of hate and anger that there was nothing more we could do. With what chain could we bind her that she could not slip through? What power could restore her honesty and put her in her right mind?

I know what the Gerasenes have been through. I knew it when I spoke to a brother after he had again broken the covenant with his wife. This time he had broken it hard—he hit his wife. It was hard for him to hear me. The only words *he* heard were the ones he used to cut himself. I listened helplessly as he scraped, scratched, and tore himself with self-accusation and damnation. With what chain could we bind him to his family? What power could restore the trust and love lost to betrayal and violence? Some of you know what the Gerasenes have been through because you, like the friends and loved ones I have mentioned, have been the demoniac. You know who you are. Some of you have known the agony of sin and evil in your soul and flesh. It has oppressed you, dehumanized you, injured you, and condemned you. You have broken the bonds of covenant and trust. You have hurt yourself and others because the power of addiction, hate, lust, and violence was too strong. Even when others tried to help, you broke through their efforts to contain the powers. You know what the Gerasenes have been through because you were the demoniac. No chain forged by friends and neighbors was able to restrain you. There seemed to be no power to restore you. There appeared to be no power stronger than the evil that hurt you.

Whether we identify with the Gerasenes or the demoniac, we have all suffered because of the power of the "Strong Man." We have been either disturbed or dehumanized by legions of evil. In our text, the demoniac and his demons ask a significant question: "What have you to do with [us], Jesus, Son of the God Most High?" This is a good question for us whether we have been "possessed by the powers" or "pestered by the possessed." Faced with our weakness and frustration before the forces of evil, we wonder what Jesus' business with us might be. Will he help? Will he judge? Will he restore? Can he restrain the work of evil? Is he stronger than the Strong Man?

Stronger than the Strong Man and His Legions

Mark's gospel tells us of an occasion prior to the one in Gerasa, when Jesus exorcised a demon in Capernaum (Mark 1:21–28). That spirit asked the same question: "What have you to do with us, Jesus of Nazareth?" Has Jesus come to destroy the evil that we have tried our best to contain? If he has, do we really believe that he can? In Capernaum, Jesus casts out a lone unclean spirit wandering into the synagogue. In Capernaum, Jesus ministers to a troubled soul who has come forward in the worship meeting.

The situation in Gerasa, however, is on a completely different scale. In Gerasa, Jesus is in an unclean land and an unclean place, a graveyard, surrounded by people who raise unclean animals, swine. In Gerasa, Jesus is met by a scarred-up, chain-busting nightmare who once was a human being. Who is this Jesus who seems no more intimidated by the powers of evil in Gerasa than he was in Capernaum? What does he have to do with the powers that possess us and pester us?

Perhaps the answer is given in the drama that unfolds on the Gerasene shore. The one whom the Gerasenes tried to contain meets Jesus. If this "Legion" was ready for battle, it was all for nothing, because Jesus skips the battle and goes directly to the negotiation of surrender:

Jesus commands, "Come out of him and leave him alone!"

"What do you have to do with us Jesus, Son of the God Most High?" replies evil.

"What's your name?" Jesus asks.

"Legion! There are many of us! We like it here. Don't make us leave!"

"You are evil, and you must go."

"What about the pigs? That's better than nothing; send us into the pigs!

"Go!" Jesus orders.

The outcome is clear. The demons are destroyed. Jesus does not even bother to restrain the man, for he intends much better; he releases him and restores him. Jesus gives him back his human self. The release and restoration are simple, but the reactions are more complicated. The demons are drowning in the sea, but their question only minutes old still hangs in the air: "What have you to do with [us], Jesus, Son of the God Most High?" The question asked by demons is now a question picked up by those who have witnessed the power of Jesus, who is stronger than the Strong Man and his Legion.

What Do You Have to Do with Us?

Jesus didn't ask the Gerasenes for permission when he gave right of way for the Legion to invade the pigs. The Son of the God Most High does not have to ask permission. Nor does he negotiate with evil. Jesus isn't interested in simply chaining, restraining, or managing evil—he intends to annihilate it. The unclean spirit in Capernaum knew this. The Legion did also. When Jesus works in our families, community, and cities to release people from the dehumanizing, humiliating, oppressive work of evil and sin, he doesn't intend to stop at chaining up the possessed and dropping them off in the cemetery.

Perhaps the Gerasenes understood the implication of this better than we do. After all, when they saw the man they tried to help all those years made fully human, they realized this stranger's power. Yet, their amazement gives way to fear, for if they couldn't restrain the Strong Man, then they certainly could not restrain the Stronger Man. They too could ask, "What have you to do with us, Jesus, Son of the God Most High?" The Gerasenes cannot ignore the inestimable good that has been done for this man who is now covering his shame and talking like an ordinary person. Yet, they also cannot ignore that such a power cannot be domesticated or controlled by their efforts. The Son of the God Most High may be good, but a herd of pig carcasses bobbing on the waves is witness that he cannot be reduced to "safe."

Do we know what the Gerasenes have been through because, like them, we are just human, or because, like them, we have asked Jesus to leave the area? A sad fact of church history is that the mission of God and the presence of Jesus Christ and the Holy Spirit are often squelched or turned away by well-intentioned but fearful people. When we are aware that the power of the God Most High cannot be contained or bottled, we are tempted to resist it. We would rather rely on our own weak and ineffective means because we are threatened by the Son of the God Most High. "We're only human!" we protest. Are we? When we surrender to fear and resist being amazed by the Son of the God Most High, are we fully human?

Go, Tell the Good News

This man fears that he will forever be known by his past. I can understand that. I have seen lives transformed and seen human dignity and human spirituality restored by Jesus, but I still "remember them when." Is it any wonder that the once-possessed Gerasene man, whose true name we never learn, wants to leave his hometown and go with Jesus? Perhaps he is concerned that he will be forever known only as "Legion." If prophets have no honor in their hometown, troubled people that everyone tried to help and restrain without success are even more despised. Yet, this man has something better than a name. He has a story. He has a mission worthy of his restored humanity: "Go tell the good news. Tell them what the Son of the God Most High had to do with you."

The Gerasenes recognized the power and authority of Jesus, but they did not recognize his goodness. This demoniac can now proclaim that to them. The lives of those who have been restored to humanity are a witness among us. They witness to the incredible power and authority of the Son of the Most High God, but also to his goodness. They show us what a human being shaped by the gospel of Jesus Christ is like. Does the gospel shape your sense of self and your identity? Do you have a good story to tell? If you know who Jesus is, then you do. And you know who you are.

12

Preaching to Power

Mark 6:14–29

JERRY ANDREW TAYLOR

Compositional Comments

One of Morna Hooker's significant insights is that Mark's gospel functions like a theater play with the parallels to contemporary Greek drama. Hooker believes that as the prologue in Greek drama was necessary to understand the play, so Mark's opening paragraphs are needed to understand his gospel. Hooker asks how the theater audience comprehends the play's plot and direction, and answers that the audience is privy to the event's meaning because they heard and saw information at the very beginning, in the play's prologue. In similar fashion, Mark tells at the beginning of his gospel how he wants us to hear his story and alerts us to particular features.

Hooker's insight led me to dismantle a system that kept Mark's prologue (1:1–13) separate and inferior to the sermon text (6:14–29). The prologue deserves respect because it provides a network of links to a number of pericopes throughout Mark, including 6:14–29. Perhaps, if the prologue stood alone as an isolated pericope, it could carry within itself the full freight of Mark's gospel. It is more beneficial, however, to view the prologue and the text as interdependently connected to one another. They are in some ways like

135

very close twins. The prologue introduces its twin and shares important features, giving us hints and clues about how to approach the text to reveal its most treasured insights.

As I developed the sermon, the prologue coached me and held me accountable, assisting me to identify relevant themes such as courage, faith, and obedience. I also consulted the prologue when seeking to make relevant applications of the textual themes. I then began to view my own sermon like a gospel drama that should contain a helpful prologue for the hearers. I sought to give hints and clues in the introduction to foreshadow and highlight key elements in the sermon, like a finger pointing to matters of special consideration. Thus, early in the sermon I want the audience to see the clear connection between the life and death of John the Baptist and the life and death of Jesus. I want to forecast that what happens to John because of his prophetic message will also happen to Jesus who walks in the way John prepared.

In the following sermon, delivered during worship before a gathering of ministers, I seek to persuade preachers of the gospel to follow faithfully in the way that Jesus has prepared for us. The sermon makes the point that as ministers of the gospel we have been called to put our necks on the line by confronting political power with prophetic truth. We may indeed end up losing our heads, but the character of prophetic preaching is indestructible. We are called to something that is eternal and ongoing.

The Sermon: Preaching to Power

John the Baptist sets a challenging example in Mark 6:14–29 for those who dare to engage in prophetic ministry today. John courageously confronts the political elite of his day with a solid rebuke of their unlawful conduct. He demonstrates how the servant of the Lord must carry out the prophetic ministry with bold actions and fearless speech. John the Baptist realizes that his bold speaking out against the king's unlawful arrangement could cost him everything, including the loss of his life. John's behavior in Mark's prologue (1:1–13) gives us insight into what prepared John to act boldly in 6:14–29. In the prologue John is portrayed as being independent of the finer things in life. He has a modest amount of this world's goods in the form of his diet and apparel. This simple lifestyle equips him to speak prophetically to those in power.

Morna Hooker makes the point that we must give special attention to Mark's beginning in order to understand the entirety of Mark's gospel. In light of Hooker's main thesis, I see Mark's gospel as a cinematic drama. It is like a movie that must be seen from the start for the viewer to have a meaningful understanding of each of its parts. At the beginning we get all the hints and clues of what to look for and what to pay special attention to throughout the movie. Without the beginning, it is very hard to follow the story line to its conclusion.

At the beginning of Mark's gospel drama, he tells us in thirteen verses what he wants us to know up front. Mark's prologue is so packed with gospel content that it could actually stand independently from the rest of the gospel and still carry in short form the full freight of Mark's entire gospel. In Mark's prologue we see the pronounced details about John the Baptist's forerunning ministry. John the Baptist is portrayed as a servant of God who knows with a burning passion his life's mission. In Mark 6:14–29 we see John carrying out his call to bear witness to truth, no matter the cost.

Today servants of the gospel are called to bear witness to the truth that Jesus Christ is Lord above all! Our mission is not to draw attention to ourselves but to point to the one who commissioned us to go into all the word proclaiming the good news. The one we proclaim as Lord is greater than ourselves. Like John the Baptist, we baptize with mere water, but our Lord baptizes with the Holy Spirit. Servants of the gospel have received the noble task of using the language of love to communicate truth to humans from every station of life. We speak truth not only to the weak and powerless. We also speak truth to those with privilege, power, and position.

Mark's prologue tells us of John the Baptist's fearless character, that he spent time alone with God in the wilderness. Today, God's servants seek to follow John's example. We, too, feel the need to spend time alone with God in the wilderness. In the unplanned wilderness, God strips us of our dependence upon order and structure. In the unpredictable wilderness, we encounter that formless silence that pulls our divided hearts away from the deadly distractions of a highly advanced world. In the wilderness, God weans us from our addiction to predictable order and settled routine. In that formless place of stillness, in the wilderness of God's holy silence, we learn to receive with meekness God's engrafted Word. Our reverence for God and God's engrafted Word causes us to be filled with an unbreakable courage that shatters every fear of corrupt power in high places. The message received in the wilderness is very dangerous because it often ends up causing servants of God to be in direct conflict with the power structure within the preplanned social arrangements of the religious and secular worlds.

John the Baptist is a brave servant of God who is not intimidated by the power structure in the king's palace. John the Baptist is courageous because he has undergone God's basic training regimen for prophets. John received the spirit and courage of the prophets of old that emboldened him to confront an illegal social arrangement that existed in the center of political power in Herod's palace. He said to King Herod, "It is not lawful for you to have your brother's wife." Our own experience teaches us that kings and political leaders aren't accustomed to being told what they cannot have! In many cases, those with power believe they are entitled to live above the requirements of the law. In our own nation we have seen presidents from both political parties expressing their strong will to have it their way, from Watergate to the Iran Contra scandal and from the Lewinsky affair to a war of mass destruction in Iraq, initiated on false and misleading information.

John's rebuke of King Herod's unlawful arrangement reminds us of Nathan's rebuke of David, and Elijah's challenge to Ahab over the death of Naboth. John's fearless condemnation of injustice and hypocrisy in high places shows that he did not treat status and power with favoritism. God's prophets can speak and act boldly because they are not dependent upon the gifts, comforts, and pleasures afforded by the powerful political institutions of the world. God's servants see these deceptive comforts as distracting bribes that are used to silence God's prophet who attempts to courageously speak truth to power.

In the prologue, Mark portrays John wearing clothing made of camel's hair, with a leather belt around his waist, eating locusts and wild honey. Camel's hair, locusts, and wild honey shall be the apparel and the diet of those who dare speak truth to power. John's lifestyle in the prologue reminds us we cannot speak truth to political institutions and at the same time expect them to celebrate and support us in a lifestyle of the rich and famous. Often our desire to live a lavish lifestyle of comfort and ease causes us to remain shamefully silent in the face of institutional evil.

John's prophetic lifestyle described in the prologue is reminiscent of the prophet Elijah's lifestyle described in 2 Kings 1:8. Herodias seems to possess the spirit of Jezebel. Jezebel hated Elijah for destroying the false prophets of Baal on Mt. Carmel, and Herodias resents John because he speaks a critical truth about Herod's unlawful relationship with her. Herodias's relationship with Herod provided her privilege and comfort in the king's palace. She could not bear the thought of the continued existence of this uncultured, politically incorrect, wilderness dweller whose speech and lifestyle interfered with her way of life.

Herodias loved her way of life so much she was willing to kill an innocent man to protect and to preserve it. She wanted John dead. Herod prevented John's immediate death, but to satisfy Herodias he had John arrested and imprisoned. Herodias, an expert at keeping a grudge alive, "nursed a grudge" against John. Even though Herod's political system prevented Herodias from immediately destroying John, Herodias's hatred and rage for John grew stronger each day. Herodias's temporary nonviolent disposition toward John was not based on a genuine practice of social tolerance for John. Herodias was being shrewd and stealthy by delaying her gratification until another day when she could get revenge against John for the painful truth he blatantly spoke against the injustice of her relationship with the king.

Herodias did not get mad about John's actions; she got *organized*. She cleverly waited until Herod's political system afforded an opportunity for her to carry out her evil plot against her targeted enemy. Herodias's actions reveal how the powerful often control political systems and manipulate them to reward their allies and to punish and destroy their perceived enemies and opponents. Herodias patiently concealed her plan of attack until Herod threw a birthday party for himself, inviting all his high officials and military commanders and the leading men of Galilee. Herodias's nameless daughter entertained the elite guests by dancing for them.

The nameless female's outstanding male-pleasing performance won for her the privilege to ask for anything she wanted from Herod, up to half his kingdom. Though this young lady won this right through her performance in a scandalous "Tail Hook" environment filled with military leaders, she did not know how to exercise the privilege extended to her. Though she had been given a token of power, she had not been properly educated in knowing how to use that power. What benefit is it to give a slave physical freedom while intentionally allowing her or him to remain enslaved within a damaged, brutalized, and unrestored intellect? What good is it to give a slave the freedom to ask for whatever she wants without first educating her about the valuable things she should ask for?

Herod's attempt to exploit the young female dancer's ignorance caused his political system to fail in educating her about what was valuable in the kingdom and how she should use her newly granted access. The failure of Herod's political system in this regard left the young female dancer vulnerable to be filled with negative and destructive information that could be given to her from any foreign source. The young female dancer turned to the only source she knew could help her figure out what to request from Herod. She consulted with her mother. She asked her mother, "What shall I ask for?" Her mother had no loving advice or wise counsel to give to her. The only thing Herodias had to give to her daughter was a well-nursed grudge. She made her daughter an accomplice in her plan of attack against John. Herodias advised her daughter to ask for the head of John the Baptist. The king's offer enabled Herodias to use the king's policy to kill John!

Herodias's daughter was an obedient child and followed her mother's evil counsel. She called for the death of an innocent man because of her mother's desires. It is sad to see that some parents' approval for their children is based upon their children's willing-ness to hate the people and groups their parents and grandparents tell them to hate. This generational transmission of hatred has been the bloody legacy left to too many children by their parents and grandparents. Too often, this infamous legacy of "hand-me-down hatred" has caused the death of many innocent people who happened to be members of racial, religious, or political groups that were earmarked as threats to unjust political arrangements.

Herod became aware that his political system was being manipulated by a grudge to kill an innocent man. Still he refused to change his course of action. Against the protest of good reason and holiness, Herod gave the order to the executioner to behead John the Baptist. Herod made this ungodly decision out of his need to impress his political base assembled in his palace. He wanted his constituency to know that he was a politician who kept his word even if it meant the destruction of an innocent life. He did not want to be accused of waffling or being indecisive!

The executioner then carries out Herod's orders in Abu Ghraib fashion. He didn't question his superiors, but like Herodias's daughter did what he was told. He knew if he had questioned the orders of the king he would have lost his own head. He probably felt it was better that someone else's head be cut off instead of his own. He probably felt justified by knowing that he was following orders so that he could excuse himself from the horror of this brutal act. How often in human history have we seen evil atrocities carried out by evil regimes all because people unthinkingly follow ungodly orders issued by their superiors? How often have we witnessed the evil mistreatment of other human beings by those who were following orders? Will the servants of God risk losing their own heads, their own income, their own reputation, and their own popularity by standing up and questioning those who give orders that conflict with God's will?

The sermon text closes on what appears to be a sad note to those unfamiliar with Mark's beginning. John the Baptist is killed, and his head is delivered to Herodias on a platter. Mark tells us, "When his disciples heard about it, they came and took his body, and laid it in a tomb" (6:29). It appeared that John's prophetic ministry had come to a tragic end. But those of us who know Mark's beginning understand that this tragic act marked the end of John's ministry, but it did not mark the end of "Truth." Those of us who know Mark's prologue understand that John served his purpose. His mission is now accomplished. He has successfully fulfilled his calling.

Now John's grieving disciples are forced to look to Jesus Christ, the one to whom John pointed. They must give up their attachment to John and become followers of Jesus. The quotation from Malachi in Mark's prologue speaks of a herald going on ahead of his king to summon people to make ready for the king's coming. This is what John did. John was a preview to the main feature. When Herod heard of the miraculous powers at work in Jesus, he thought John the Baptist had returned from the dead. Herod was not privy to the information we are given in the prologue. He could not read the beginning of Mark's gospel drama because he is a character in the drama. But we are privileged to be able to read the beginning, to see the gospel drama in its entirety.

- If Herod only knew what we know from reading Mark's beginning, he would have understood that John the Baptist was only a precursor to the real Word known as Christ.

- If Herod had known Mark's prologue, he would have known that John the Baptist said in Mark 1:7 "The one who is more powerful than I is coming after me; I am not worthy to stoop down and untie the thong of his sandals."

- If Herod had known Mark's beginning, he would have known that John said in Mark 1:8, "I have baptized you with water, but he will baptize you with the Holy Spirit."

- If Herod had known Mark's prologue, he would have known that John proclaimed truth, but Jesus is the Truth.

- If Herod had known Mark's beginning, he would have known that John's ministry was the ministry of repentance, but Jesus' ministry is the ministry of conversion.
- If Herod had known Mark's prologue, he would have known that John was a messenger, but Jesus is the Message!
- He would have known that prophets of God may face a very bitter end, but there is no end to the "Truth" they proclaim!
- Herod would have known that the state's ultimate weapon of mass control—which is death—could not prevent the triumphant march of God's will in the world.
- Herod would have known that servants of God already know that when they speak the truth about unlawful social arrangements in the empire the empire will strike back.

But God's servants also know that kings may cut off the heads of prophets, but kings do not have the power to cut off the voice of Truth. Truth is relentless and unyielding.

Empires that once despised and brutally raped Truth in the public square have now fallen in humiliating collapse at the feet of Truth.

Though public opinion is often intolerant of Truth, Truth still remains the greatest public defender against the brutality of tyranny.

Political empires have bruised the beautiful face of Truth with the ugly fists of manipulative deception, but Truth's beauty is still more captivating than a million sunsets.

In the political houses of Congress, the politics of self-interests have sold the seat reserved for Truth to big money donors. It may appear that Truth gets tired of standing, but she continues to stand up for that which is right.

The present hour is pregnant with the need for God's servants who are more committed to speaking the mega-Truth than they are to building mega-ministries.

The soul of America is growing darker and darker each day in the absence of Truthful speech. God bless America, and God bless the servants of God who must speak Truth to and within America.

God bless us with the courage of John the Baptist to put our necks on the line by speaking Truth to those who hold the power to destroy us in every way.

We thank you God for the prophetic message you have given us in the silent wilderness of your awesome Presence. Grant us now the courage to preach your challenging word to our well-structured society that often places itself above your Will. We know you are with us as you were with the faithful prophets of old who spoke your word to the political elite of their day and paid the ultimate price with their very lives. We are grateful to be counted worthy to be in the company of the persecuted who are hated, despised, and persecuted for your name's sake.

13

Only the Blind Can See

Mark 8:22–26

JOHN YORK

Compositional Comments

John York preached this sermon at the 2005 Rochester Sermon Seminar to an audience of over two hundred seasoned preachers. After the sermon, Mel Storm, who teaches New Testament at Rochester College and serves as an elder for the Heritage Church of Christ in Clawson, Michigan, and Dave Bland offered a critique of the sermon, with John responding. John crafted his sermon with the Rochester audience in mind and thus uses examples and images that relate well to the academy and to the professional preacher. However, this sermon can and will generate ideas for adapting a similar message to other audiences.

One of the ways the sermon engages the listener is through the use of a series of tensions. John plays on a number of ironies embedded within the story. (1) It takes Jesus two attempts to heal the blind man. What's with that? (2) The blind man is the only one who can really see. (3) We find ourselves chastising the disciples because they don't get it, only to be jolted into the realization that we are just as blind as they. By highlighting these ironies the sermon breaks down our defenses and leads us on the path to humility before the Christ.

In this sermon John uses a strong narrative movement that incorporates the whole discourse on discipleship in Mark 8—10.

The sermon ties the healing of the blind man with Peter's confession at Caesarea Philippi that immediately follows. As a result we gain new insight and experience an "aha moment": The blind man only saw stick men; the disciples could only recognize their cultural stick-figure of Messiah. The sermon also connects this story with the healing of blind Bartimaeus, thus framing the discourse on discipleship with two healing stories.

John concludes his sermon by confronting us with that which is a major visual impairment of our understanding of Christ today. John subtly invites us as preachers to first take the logs out of our own eyes before proceeding to proclaim this story to others.

The Sermon: Only the Blind Can See

In my early professor days, I often taught the beginning Greek classes. I'm sure I was as insufferable to the students in my classes as some of them were to me. It was hard work, and many of the freshmen counseled to enroll in the course had no desire to do all the memorization and the tedious, overdone Greek-to-English/English-to-Greek exercises constantly assigned.

Alas, what I discovered in myself and in every student was that a little bit of Greek was considerably worse than no Greek at all! When it comes to interpreting scripture, I realized that it doesn't get any better—or worse—than being a second-year Greek student. There is that notion of arrival when you finish reading through John's gospel. Only later does it become so painfully clear that to be able to translate the Greek words of John's gospel has so little to do with actually understanding the gospel of John. Needless to say, my track record at creating Greek scholars was not great. Part of that was no doubt due to the fact that I had lost some passion for the subject myself by the time I was teaching it. I once thought, as a student at least, that if a person just knew his or her Greek New Testament, the questions of meaning would all be solved. But then came the realization that with knowledge, more is always less. The more you think you know, the more you realize you don't know!

I suppose that is why, the older I get, the more I am drawn to the stories and the people in the gospel of Mark. In Mark's story no one ever knows anything! Yes, God knows; Jesus knows; the author seems to know; even the implied reader is supposed to know. But the characters in the story are hopelessly awash in not knowing. The disciples never figure it out in this story. Some obvious outsiders in the story, particularly the demon-possessed, recognize Jesus; but they are always quickly silenced. Other outsiders, such as the religious and political leaders—the Pharisees, Herodians, Sadducees, priests, and lawyers—always know just enough to be suspicious or downright dangerous. But those who are actually expected to know the true identity of Jesus, those invited to have insider status, invariably are seen to be ignorant. Jesus' family thinks he's crazy; his hometown is clueless; his closest associates see him perform miracles, but seem always surprised by what happens next. They puzzle over the meaning of his parables even as he tells them they are the ones with ears to hear. And, of course, if any hint of the true identity of Jesus surfaces, Jesus silences the testimony before it starts. The mystery of Messiah is to be kept secret!

It is no accident that this odd two-stage miracle story involving a blind man comes at exactly the midpoint in Mark's gospel. Nor is it by accident that the context has to do with what Jesus' closest associates, the twelve disciples, see and perceive in their travels with Jesus. The episodes immediately preceding this story feature Jesus feeding the four thousand—apparently a crowd of Gentiles— with seven loaves and a few fish, just as he had earlier fed a crowd of Jews with five loaves and two fish. Following that scene, unbelieving Pharisees confront Jesus and test him by demanding a sign. Although Jesus already has performed signs and miraculous deeds in numerous settings, he refuses to grant their request because it is borne out of distrust and disbelief rather than faith.

At this moment Jesus gets in a boat with his disciples. As they make their way across the Sea of Galilee, Jesus warns them of the yeast of the Pharisees and Herod. The disciples, however, are worried that they forgot to bring food for the trip. Although they've been with Jesus all of those months and twice experienced miraculous feedings in Jesus' presence, they don't understand or believe that with only one loaf, Jesus could sustain them. So Jesus questions them in an obvious and almost condescending way.

With all of our expertise and Christian experience, *we* know. *We* have listened to these stories long enough to see and hear the echoes that carry us from one episode to the next. *We* can't believe the disciples are so dense that they can't see and perceive or hear and understand. *We*'ve seen and heard about feeding five thousand, and *we* expected the disciples to "get it" when Jesus wanted to feed the four thousand. It seems so obvious to *us* that the unbelief of the Pharisees and Herod is still at work in the disciples. These supposed intimate associates of Jesus understand Jesus better than the Pharisees, better than Jesus' own relatives, and better than his hometown of Nazareth. They realize he is a great miracle worker, but have not ears to hear, nor eyes to see. The disciples know he has power over wind and wave, but fail to fully understand who he is.

Which lands us on the northern shore of the Sea of Galilee in the town of Bethsaida. There are great similarities between this story and one earlier when Jesus heals the deaf man with the speech impediment (7:32-35). (1) In both stories a crowd brings to Jesus a person who has an infirmity that pushes that person to society's margins. (2) In each case the crowd begs Jesus to heal the man. (3) In each case Mark's reading audience accompany Jesus and the person away from the crowd. (4) In the first case Jesus spits and touches the man, who is healed. But the blind man is *partially* healed. It's the only miracle of its kind in the recorded life of Jesus— a two-stage miracle. When Jesus asks him if he sees anything, he reports that he sees, but the people look like walking trees. Only after Jesus touches him a second time does he see clearly. Why the two-stage miracle? Why didn't the man see clearly after the first touch? It is not a question of Jesus being unable to instantly heal the blind in Mark; he'll later heal a blind man immediately, by the spoken word, alone.

Now the scene shifts to Caesarea Philippi, where Jesus asks the disciples what they think other people see when they look at Jesus. *We* know this story. The answers all have to do with perceiving Jesus to be some kind of prophet. Some people think Jesus is John the Baptist; others believe he is Elijah. Some compare Jesus to other prophets of old. Jesus asks the disciples, "Who do you say that I am?" Peter replies, "You are the Messiah"—not a prophetic forerunner to the Christ, but Messiah himself. Jesus instantly warns them not to say anything of this to anyone else. Then he begins to reveal Messiah's true identity, "The Son of Man must undergo great suffering, and be rejected by the elders, the chief priests, and the scribes, and be killed, and after three days rise again" (8:31). But that's not the Christ Peter is expecting. That's not the Christ Peter recognizes. Peter takes Jesus aside and rebukes the one he has just confessed to be God's anointed. With all of the disciples looking on, Jesus responds, "Get behind me, Satan! For you are setting your mind not on divine things but on human things" (8:33).

But how can that be? Didn't Peter correctly identify Jesus as the Christ? This prediction of the suffering death of the Messiah[1] is met with the disciples' clueless misunderstanding and argument over personal greatness and honor. All of the ways of seeing and knowing the Messiah create the same problem as the blind receiving partial sight. Each time Jesus announces that he must suffer and die in Jerusalem, we overhear the disciples hopelessly lost in conversation about their own version of a messianic community that creates power, position, and greatness. The language of taking up a cross's shame and humiliation and losing life to save it is completely lost on them. The blind man sees stick men; the disciples only recognize their cultural stick-figure Messiah. At the midpoint in Mark's gospel, the two-stage healing of a blind man is not just another miracle story; it is a parable that depicts the struggle of everyone who thinks he or she already sees, perceives, hears, and understands Jesus the Messiah's identity.

What is so intriguing about Mark's story is that we get all the way to the end—to the inevitable cross event. We hear of resurrection, and recognition by women that the tomb is empty. But knowing is still up for grabs! *We* are left with the mystery of women afraid to speak what they have seen and heard. *We—you and I*—are the resurrection witnesses.

More than once in this volume, we are directed to the one instance in which sight is fully given. In contrast to the blind man from Bethsaida stands the story of blind Bartimaeus, who sees Jesus clearly *before* he receives physical sight. That is the power of his testimony—"Jesus, Son of David, have mercy on me!" (10:48). In his physical blindness he utters words of spiritual (in)sight. Bartimaeus is rewarded. "Your faith has made you well," Jesus says, and the man follows Jesus down the road. He sees! Ah, but does he?

I sometimes wonder today about the clarity of our vision, don't you? For all of the clarity and precision of the historical-critical method, text criticism, social-scientific criticism, narrative theology, and even inductive preaching, the complaints ring out in our land that the Messiah has been replaced by Christendom—that the made-in-God's-image humanity Jesus came to restore has lost out yet again to modern brands of Pharisaism, exclusivity, and political power brokerage in the name of bringing *God back to America*. I don't know about you, but the more clearly people claim to see and know Jesus, the more I want to run in the other direction as hard and fast as I can.

Too often the modern construct of the Messiah looks exactly as it did to the early disciples—an opportunity for greatness. A chance to separate the haves and have-nots, a means to power and the announcement of doom to the powerless. Rather than justice and mercy and the end of oppression, the end of bigotry and racism and difference making, our churches become havens for maintaining our material elitism or our baby empires called mega-churches. Rather than following Jesus to the cross of shame and even death, our crosses are made of the finest gold and silver, our fish symbols attached to our cultural arrival symbols—luxury SUV's, and our cultural complaint driven by the need to get gas prices back under $2 a gallon. We often are far more passionate about winning and losing in sports than we are about saving people's lives. And the truth about sports in my community is that the Tennessee Titans have done more to integrate our city than our churches ever dreamed possible.

I think Mark may be onto something in his presentation of Jesus and his parabolic use of this story. Perhaps only those who know they are blind have any opportunity of seeing at all. And only those who finally recognize that what they at first thought was sight turned out to be just stick-figure faith have any chance of that second touch. Perhaps it is not about knowing, but about admitting all that abides in mystery. To know may mean that we know too much, which is not to know at all. How painful to make that discovery in a culture so self-assured, in church cultures so attached to right answers and right performances. Like women who have been to the empty tomb and heard the voice of that young man dressed all in white telling us to go and tell, we need to be stunned to silence.

Listen! I think in the margins of the room, I just heard someone say, "Jesus, Son of David, have mercy on me!"

14

Radical Discipleship

Mark 8:31–38

DAVE BLAND

Compositional Comments

In chapter 6 of this volume, John Barton speaks of the different kinds of Jesuses we create. We, like Thomas Jefferson, tend to cut away those portions of scripture that make us uncomfortable and threaten our secure lifestyle. Referring to the text from which I develop this sermon, Barton puts it this way:

> Of course, Mark knows something about the tailor-made–Jesus business. He had heard too many stories from Peter about his struggle with such issues. You can almost hear Jesus rebuking Peter: "Get behind me, Satan!" and, "You do not have in mind the concerns of God, but merely human concerns," and, "Whoever wants to be my disciple must deny themselves and take up their cross and follow me." Understood in the context of Mark's narrative, I think Jesus told Peter: "Peter, your cut-and-paste version of me will not do. In fact, something about it is demonic. But it's a start. I can still work with it. Now stay with me on the road, and we will continue to transform you and your images of me."

For Barton the most pertinent question is not, Are we guilty of creating Jesus in our own image? because he rightly observes that we all are guilty. Rather, the question is, Are we on the road with Jesus? Are we journeying with Jesus to Jerusalem? This sermon seeks to explore that question.

The Sermon: Radical Discipleship

An article appeared in *Newsweek* a couple of years ago describing a new style of backpacking.[1] It takes all the sweat, pain, hard work, and discomfort out of it. For a price, you can hire an outfitting company to do all the work, the cooking, the carrying of equipment and backpacks, the setting up of camp, while you can just enjoy the scenic views. It eliminates the inconveniences, hardships, and hazards, leaving you to really enjoy the outdoors. You can have the joys without the grief! It's called "Back Country Lite."

Churches are tempted to produce a similar type of "Christianity Lite." It takes all the pesky inconveniences and demands out of Christianity. That way you can really enjoy Christianity. You can participate in a few activities here and there; you can sing and worship without feeling the need to accept its burden. Your life doesn't need to change. In other words, Christianity is customized to fit your lifestyle so it's more manageable; it doesn't get in the way of your own agenda.

What a contrast to Jesus' call to discipleship in Mark's gospel! As Jesus nears the end of his ministry, he turns his attention away from the crowds and focuses in on his disciples, educating them about who he is and what it means to follow him. The moment of truth finally arrives in Caesarea Philippi. Jesus asks the disciples, "Who do people say that I am?" (8:27).

Having kept their ears to the ground in their travels with Jesus, they inform him, "Some say you are John the Baptist, some say you're Elijah, and others say you are one of the prophets."

"But who do you say that I am?"

Peter, confident of his insightfulness, pronounces, "You are the Messiah!" Eureka! The disciples finally articulate Jesus' identity. After three years, their eyes are finally opened—but not completely. Their perception of what it means to be Messiah is jaded with cultural baggage. As Jesus journeys toward Jerusalem, he must peel away the misconceptions and penetrate to the heart of what it means to be Messiah. Jesus begins to teach them, "The Son of Man must undergo great suffering…" He continues, "I must suffer, and be rejected by the elders, the chief priests, and the scribes, and be killed, and after three days rise again. Anyone who follows after me must deny themselves and take up their cross."

But Peter doesn't get it, "What do you mean, Lord? They can't kill you! You will set up a new earthly rule. You will defeat this evil political system, and we will serve beside you in your reign of justice and implement your new righteous policies!" The last thing Peter wants to hear is that his king will suffer and die.

From my perspective, Jesus' agenda of suffering and dying just doesn't make sense either. After all, these days it's ridiculous to die for your faith. What would you gain by doing that? I would have rebuked him, too, because those who die for their faith are those who are the mindless fanatics! We know about these kinds of crazy people.

During the tragic aftermath of the Heaven's Gate suicides in California, a reporter appeared outraged that a group of people in contemporary America would still willingly die for religion. A preacher responded to the reporter's repudiation of the act, "A curious thing in my congregation is that almost nobody has given his or her life for religion. And yet, in the past year, I've had a half-dozen people either die or come near death with heart attacks, high blood pressure, and other diseases brought on by stress related to work. In our society, you are considered crazy if you give your life for your faith, but you are considered normal if you drop dead for a dollar!"[2] If you die for your religious beliefs, you are labeled a lunatic. Yes, I think I would have rebuked Jesus.

Jesus turns and rebukes Peter, using the occasion as an opportunity to clarify further what it means to follow the Christ: "If any want to become my followers, let them deny themselves and take up their cross and follow me. For those who want to save their life will lose it, and those who lose their life for my sake, and for the sake of the gospel, will save it" (8:34–35). Radical discipleship demands a thoroughgoing transformation. It implies fanaticism. This discipleship is demanding! I sympathize with the disciples' misunderstanding. Discipleship is a costly enterprise to undertake. I would try any way I could to misunderstand what Jesus means! A recent book entitled *Mere Discipleship* argues that we as a church have taken discipleship out of Christianity. We've made Christianity user-friendly, removing many of its rough edges, its demands, and its hard sayings so that we can live as "Christians" without changing our lifestyles. We domesticate the rhetoric of Christianity to make it more palatable so as not to embarrass good churchgoing folks. It reminds me of a scene from *Huckleberry Finn* when Huck comes to live with the Grangerfords for a while. At the time the Grangerfords are feuding with another family, the Shepherdsons. These two families have been fighting each other for thirty years.

When Sunday rolls around, Huck finds himself going to church with all the Grangerfords and the Shepherdsons. The men take their guns into the building and stand them between their knees or prop them against the wall within convenient reach.

The sermon that day is all about brotherly love. Huck observes, "It was pretty ornery preaching—all about brotherly love, and such-like tiresomeness." On the way home everybody talked about how the sermon "had such a powerful lot to say about faith and good works and free grace and preforeordestination" and a bunch of other stuff Huck didn't understand. Yet come Monday morning everyone went back to fussing and feuding and fighting.

We like sermons on grace and brotherly love. We've got the Christian speech and language down. Yet the church frequently develops a generic brand of what at least one person has called "undiscipled disciples."[3] In this brand of discipleship, giving, for example, becomes a mathematical equation rather than a heartfelt offering. Prayer becomes an issue of time management instead of a spiritual quest. Serving others is mostly random and treated as an opportunity to put another notch on the spiritual belt rather than something that flows out of a deeply embedded lifestyle. We've developed a Christianity without discipleship. Christianity loses the emphasis on discipleship and replaces it with an emphasis upon religious ritual that allots only certain times to practice it. Its radical nature is removed.

Later, as Jesus and the disciples journey closer to Jerusalem, Jesus finds another opportunity to speak to the disciples about his destiny: "They will betray me and kill me. But in three days I will rise again." The whole time he is saying this, the disciples are arguing among themselves, "Who among us is going to be the greatest?" Jesus instructs the twelve: "Whoever wants to be great must be servant of all" (9:30–35). Such a perspective is life-changing and risky because it involves a radical change in priorities. We are tempted to trivialize Christianity. We want to make sure we can keep our lives intact. We use Christianity to promote our well-being, our comfortable lifestyle. Our recipe for discipleship is much like customizing the ingredients for spaghetti sauce to our own liking. Put in a cup of tomato paste, add a little bit of oregano, then a pinch of garlic, a sprinkle of thyme and basil, and flavor it with onion. You can include or exclude whatever you want in any amount that you want.

We create a discipleship that suits our taste. Attach a little worship to the weekend, add a pinch of prayer to each day, and patch on a service project now and then. Occasionally participate in a mission trip. You can add these spiritual activities while at the same time keeping your life intact. We've made Christianity a list of optional ingredients.

Just before Jesus enters Jerusalem, he takes one final opportunity to announce his suffering and death and what that means for those who would follow him. James and John flippantly respond with a request, "Lord, can we have the choice seats in your new kingdom? Can we sit to the immediate right and left of you?" Once again Jesus reminds them: "Whoever wishes to become great among you must be your servant...For the Son of Man came not to be served but to serve" (10:43b, 45a). He who is greatest, he who is a disciple, Jesus said, is the servant. Discipleship equals servanthood. But we want to be the powerbrokers, the movers and shakers, not a suffering servant. Jesus continually rebuked his disciples for believing that politics was where the world would get changed. Jesus said it's the servant role.

Our culture prefers power and control to the servant role. We prefer "the rod to the reed."[4] We assume that to make significant cultural changes we must do so from the top down. Jesus taught the opposite. He told his disciples not to get a hold of political power but to grasp servanthood. In Mark's gospel it is not the scribes, leaders, or teachers of the law who grasp servanthood. It is the sick, the Gentiles, and the women.

Who has greater power, a thousand people filling the streets to protest abortion in front of an abortion clinic, or a thousand people lined up to adopt unwanted children of whatever race or physical condition? Who has stronger influence, those who lobby the federal government to give more financial aid in the aftermath of Katrina and Rita or those who set up shelters for the evacuees in their homes and churches? Who makes a more lasting impression, those who send financial aid to New Orleans or those who travel to that city to help the residents rebuild? Whose work will reap more enduring benefits, the one who campaigns for stricter gun control or the one who volunteers as a "Big Brother"? Discipleship and service are synonymous and costly.

Yet Jesus is patient with his disciples as they seek to understand what it means to follow him. Fully committing to Christ is not a lifestyle acquired instantaneously or even naturally. Rather, by the leading of the Spirit, you learn and grow in the discipline of discipleship. Discipleship is a journey, a process of transformation. All through the period of time the disciples travel with Jesus, they never quite get what Jesus is about. But Jesus takes them as they are, misunderstandings and all, and nurtures them along the way, sometimes with gentleness and sometimes with strong rebuke. He takes whoever would follow him just as they are and molds them into his disciples, similar to a coach tapping into the raw talent of a young woman learning to play the game of basketball. With rigor, discipline, and patience the coach develops her into a skilled athlete.

After his resurrection, Jesus invites his disciples, failures and all, to follow him again to Galilee. Jesus will not give up on them. Discipleship is a learning process, and the learning curve is steep. The teacher, though demanding, practices forbearance and love in introducing us to the way discipleship manifests itself in everyday life, even in the seemingly insignificant decisions we make and relationships we encounter. Discipleship involves practicing integrity, even when it costs. It means investing ourselves in the lives of others: listening to a friend share her pain, being there for one struggling with depression, giving your time and energy to help a single parent, being present for one experiencing loss, preparing a meal for a new family in the neighborhood, or writing cards of encouragement. Discipleship involves small acts of kindness.

Discipleship takes on different forms for different people. Even for the same person, it demands different responsibilities on different occasions. For some it may involve a redirection of time and energy away from certain hobbies and toward family or friends or community. Still for others it might require a change in personal relationships or a commitment of financial resources. It may mean telling a friend engaged in adultery that God is not pleased with his or her actions. It may mean discussing the destructive behavior of a friend or family member at the risk of that person's rejection. For some it might go so far as to necessitate a change in vocation.

Millard Fuller spoke to a group of college students at Duke University a few years back. He told them about how he and his wife prayerfully decided to sell everything they had, leave a successful law practice, move to a poor neighborhood in Americus, Georgia, and see what doors opened for serving the poor in that community. The result was that they started building houses for poor people, and thus Habitat for Humanity was born. After Fuller spoke on that occasion, several in the audience inquired about the Fuller's children: How old were they when they moved, and how did the move affect them? Did this move really consider their needs? Behind the questions was this concern: It's fine if parents want to make a sacrifice for a religious commitment that they want to experience. But it's not fine to drag your children into it with you, uproot their lives, and ask them to sacrifice for the parents' values. Here's the irony: Don't all parents sacrifice their children to their own values?[5]

Many of our values may be wrongheaded. We may hold to a number of misunderstandings about what kind of Messiah Jesus really is. But the important question is, "Are we at least heading in the same direction as Jesus?" Are we willing to travel with him to Galilee?

15

Do You See What I See?

Mark 9:1–9

SPENCER FURBY

Compositional Comments

Sometimes a simple hermeneutic observation leads to profound homiletic results. The insight Fred Craddock provides concerning the reader of Mark is one such instance. The reader is made privy to private events and conversations, allowing the reader to actually be in the gospel story as it progresses. It leads us to understand that Mark's purpose was to invite us into the story. This simple perspective provided the imaginative spark for this sermon, as seen in the present tense of the verbs and the concluding observation that the stories incorporated were chosen for *our* benefit—to accomplish Mark's purpose *in us*.

The sermon also bears witness to the contributions of Hooker to the study of Mark. She notes that the first thirteen verses stand apart from the rest of the book. Insights found there are shared with us but not with the characters in the story, a possible clue and affirmation of Craddock's insight. This section provides information necessary to understand the rest of the story, as evidenced by the "links" that are carried forward to other parts of it. Hooker says that the prologue "points us to a deeper understanding of his message" and through it Mark "challenges us to share his belief in the good news about Jesus Christ." For this reason I use the image of optometry as the connective tissue sustaining the movement of the sermon and refer to the first thirteen verses as the "wall chart."

But the epilogue is of the same essence. The book ends abruptly and mysteriously, forcing us to speculate about Mark's purpose. "The stark conclusion forces us to think and act," Hooker says, and "invites us to decide what will come next." Hooker argues that John in the prologue is summoning us to see Jesus as the Christ and follow him, while the young man in the tomb at the conclusion is surely addressing us to see and follow as well. But we are left stranded, wondering what the disciples did in response. Hooker calls this a "brilliant strategy," for only if the disciples obeyed in faith would they see Jesus, and the same is true for us. By ending Mark with the women's reaction, Mark reminds us of the importance of our response. What are we going to do?

This sermon seeks to incorporate the prologue and conclusion as an *inclusio* for the message. Out of this understanding, the transfiguration is seen as a vital link in the book, affirming the insights provided in the prologue and looking forward to the conclusion anticipated (but not completely provided) by the epilogue. The imagery of vision is comprehensive enough to keep intact the linkage Mark was striving for throughout the book, providing a holistic treatment faithful to Mark's purpose. Mark's goal was to lead the reader to believe, obey, and see Jesus, in that order. That is the goal of our preaching as well.

The Sermon: Do You See What I See?

Mark is an optometrist. His job through the gospel is to get us to see who Jesus is. He assumes that when we witness the evidence, clear vision of the identity of Jesus will result. I remember how unpleasant a trip to the optometrist (as a child) was. Unlike going to the dentist, we only went to the optometrist if a problem was suspected. He would shine the light in my eyes and dilate them to a terribly uncomfortable state. He would stick the series of lenses over my eyes. As I answered how far down on the chart I could read, he would *click* another lens down over the others. The entire time I was there I heard *click! click! click!* as he tried to determine my quality of vision. Of course, glasses were needed.

For the gospel of Mark, the first 13 verses function as the wall chart, providing the truth that Mark wants us to see. "Jesus is the Christ," Mark says. He writes everything else to confirm that. He begins with the point of reference, the 20/20 result he wants us to get to. But only we readers know about the chart. The characters in the story are ignorant of the conclusion already announced. Mark then introduces the stories he thinks should clarify for the characters, and especially the disciples, who Jesus is. Each story serves as a *click!* that, when taken in totality, will lead to people seeing the chart clearly. John the Baptist was a prophet, Mark says in the wall chart passage, who spoke for all of the Old Testament in saying that this Jesus is the one who was promised, and that we should listen to and follow him. If Mark does his job as optometrist well, the characters should eventually view Jesus clearly as the Christ and listen to him.

This approach of Mark is made parabolically clear in the story about the blind man in Mark 8. Jesus touches the blind man. Jesus, himself acting as an optometrist, has taken the blind man aside. In the privacy of his office Jesus does some work with him and empowers him to see. "Now, sir, can you see clearly?" Jesus asked.

"Well, not exactly. I see people, and I am thrilled about that. But they are still a little blurry and look like trees, sort of." So Jesus touches him again, and the man shouts out joyfully that all is clear. More than one *click!* is necessary.

We are to understand this story as an outline for the book. The first half is about getting the disciples to see *who* Jesus is. The second half is about getting them to accept *what* he is to do. When the scene progresses to the disciples near Caesarea Philippi, Jesus acts as an optometrist to them. "When it comes to what I have done, whom do people see me as?" he asks the apostles.

They give him a survey. "Well, some people see you as John the Baptist. Some see you as Elijah. Some see you as an Old Testament prophet."

"Okay. I can see why they would think so. But you are my disciples. Whom do you see me as?"

They think about it, and Peter speaks for them. "You are the Christ." So Jesus now knows that the *clicks!* provided so far have made his first job successful. The first touch has been good. But how clearly do they see him? He puts the prophetic description of the work of the Christ before them, the suffering and death and resurrection. Peter rebukes him. This description is not what Peter sees for the Christ. It is obvious that he needs further treatment. He has vision, but it is blurry. You do not rebuke the Christ of God. Jesus now knows he has more work to do. So starts part 2 of the work of Mark, more *clicks!* to increase accuracy of vision.

The scene shifts, but Mark wants us to know that the new scene is related in purpose to the scene just shared. Jesus waits six days after Peter's confession and rebuke. Jesus knows he needs to work immediately on the situation because blurriness is often worse than blindness. Blurriness is interpreted as clear sight and leads to tragic mistakes. Something has to happen to help clear it up. So he takes Peter, James, and John up on a mountain alone and is transfigured before them. He glowed and was joined by Moses and Elijah. When Peter looked up and saw the sight before him, he was terrified. He saw Jesus as the Christ; but when this Christ was placed beside familiar authoritative figures, Peter was quite unsettled as to what to think and do. So he offers to build three shelters. Why? No one knows. Maybe even Peter didn't know. But you say strange things when what you see confuses you. Blurriness is disturbing when you experience the inevitable confusion. But it is a necessary confusion that can lead to correction, allowing a whole new world to develop before you.

His understanding is clouded, and quite fittingly God moves a cloud over them. God takes his turn as optometrist for these three disciples when he declares without confusion who Jesus is. "This is my Son, the Beloved; listen to him!" (9:7). Then the cloud disappears. Only Jesus remains. God is trying to clear up the view of Jesus for the disciples. Did it work? Well, not yet. It is going to take more time and a few more *clicks!* for them to get it. Jesus knows this. He knows that simply seeing is not enough. Understanding must come, too. So he tells the disciples not to mention what happened to anyone *until the Son of Man has risen from the dead*. The only thing more dangerous than blindness is partial vision.

I was in Rochester, Michigan, recently. A friend of mine and I toured the Leader Dogs for the Blind Institute. We were shown the dogs and taken through the process of how blind people are matched with dogs to help them maneuver in life. I asked the man if it is difficult to train people to rely on the dog. He said it sometimes was. The most difficult people to train for Seeing Eye dogs are people who have limited vision. They may be legally blind, but they still see a little. Because they can see a little bit, they rely on the little they see rather than on the dog trained to be their eyes. A blind person can only rely on the dog; a legally blind but partially seeing person can see enough to trust themselves over the dog. They just don't take full advantage. Training and teaching then become difficult. Jesus found this to be true as well. Peter got the idea of his identity down, but being able to train him in God's way for the Christ was something different. Even after God tried to clarify, it was going to take some work. But Peter seems humbled enough by the event on the mountain to open his mind to further learning.

The reference to the resurrection moves us forward to the ending of Mark. We are prompted to wonder, Do the disciples ever really see him? A mysterious man in the tomb informs us that Jesus has risen. Instruction is given to the women at the tomb. "But go, tell his disciples and Peter that he is going ahead of you to Galilee; there you will *see* him, just as he told you." But the women, at least initially, did not obey. That is where the story ends. We are left wondering, Did Mark get the job done? Did the disciples finally see clearly who Jesus was? Did the chart on the wall ever come into clear focus for the characters in the story? Mark doesn't say. Then we realize that as much as the disciples are the patients in Mark's office, so are we. Do we see Jesus clearly?

But Mark's job is not done when we simply see Jesus. Seeing Jesus will lead to obeying Jesus. The conclusion at the beginning declared Jesus to be the Christ. It showed John declaring that Jesus would baptize with the Holy Spirit. The heavenly voice identified him as the Son of God. Mark believes that people should see him that way and then listen to him. Peter is rebuked for seeing him but not listening to him. God then gets into the story and helps Peter and James and John and us to see him and understand that seeing him should lead to listening to him. At the end, the women are told that Jesus is all he said he was. He is waiting for his disciples. The women are commanded to go and tell and meet, and then they will see. The goal is not just to see Jesus. Seeing is great, but it must lead to obedience. Will the women finally see Jesus? Will the disciples finally see Jesus? If they obeyed, they did. Do we see Jesus?

16

A "Mitey" Strange Giving Analysis

Mark 12:41–44

MARK HENDERSON

Compositional Comments

The following sermon is a modification of a sermon I preached to my congregation on January 20, 2002. Two weeks earlier, I had preached a sermon that outlined "opportunities and obstacles" in the New Year. One of the obstacles focused on an analysis of congregational giving in 2001. I had really let them have it. Almost as soon as the sermon was over, this story of the widow's mite started playing in my mind. I saw much more to the business of giving analysis than I learned from the numbers on a printout.

I have incorporated Morna Hooker's observations about this passage in her commentary on Mark's gospel. She notes the contrast between this generous widow and the greedy teachers of the law who devour widows' houses, and she sees the widow as an exemplar of the disciple who embraces the two great commands.

Fred Craddock encourages allusions to scripture that respect the congregation's knowledge and memory. I tied the widow and her gift to the Christ hymn in Philippians chapter 2 without citing the passage, trusting the church to make the connection. Craddock is one of the masters at giving voice to the characters in the text, and I have attempted to do the same with my imaginary conversation with the widow in the final move of the sermon. A final "Craddockian" influence is the closing, in which I leave myself and the congregation to continue struggling with questions that defy easy answers.

The Sermon: A "Mitey" Strange Giving Analysis

Jesus sat down opposite the place where the offerings were put and watched the crowd putting their money into the temple treasury. Many rich people threw in large amounts. But a poor widow came and put in two very small copper coins, worth only a fraction of a penny. I'm glad that Jesus is paying attention to what is happening here because it seems that there are always these gross inequities in giving to the Lord's work. Twenty percent of the people give eighty percent of the money. About half the people who claim church membership and who come to receive the ministry of the church give nothing, or next to nothing. These gifts to the temple treasury were important. They provided for the upkeep of the temple and for the temple priests and their families. Those gifts also provided public support for people in need. These rich people and their large gifts are making all of that possible. Then, Jesus sees this widow. She puts in a couple of coins that are so small in value that they have funny names. The Greeks called them *lepta*. In charades, they would say, "Sounds like 'leper.'" In the *King James Version*, they are two mites. You want to say, "Why bother? You probably need them worse than we do." I'm glad Jesus is watching. It is important to do this sort of giving analysis from time to time because you always seem to have a few people paying most of the freight.

I mentioned to you two weeks ago that we had done a giving analysis of our member families for 2001. I thought that would be helpful information as we try to finish our budget process for 2002, and it was helpful! Many of you weren't here that Sunday, so I want to spend just a minute or so to review the results of that report. We had 666 family units, which I found unsettling without any further analysis. We had five families who together gave 19 percent of our giving. To make the cut for that group, you had to give over $25,000, and the top two families gave more than $50,000! Fifty-five family units gave almost 51 percent of the total. Everybody in that group gave more than $6,000 to the general fund last year. And then 20 percent of our families gave almost 75 percent of our total giving. Someone asked me where the cutoff was for that group. The 20 percent represents everyone who gave more than $3,250 to the regular contribution last year. I would like to have some more of those kinds of families, especially that top five, because they obviously understand what it means to support the ministry of the church. In fact, when I shared this data with the church a couple of weeks ago, I mentioned how grateful I was for those five families because they had not only been blessed with abundant resources, but God had also given them hearts of generosity.

Of course, the other data in that report were not so encouraging. I'll remind you that 317 family units, about 48 percent of the total, gave 1.7 percent of the total dollars. That group includes those who gave less than $500 to the general fund last year. Of those, 190 family units (28.5 percent of the total) gave nothing to the general fund last year. If you were here, you will remember that I interpreted that data for you, too. I said that I was shocked and concerned—and even a little bit frightened. After all, how can we expect God to bless us while we demonstrate such faithlessness and spiritual immaturity in our giving? I thought it was important to let you know what we had discovered in that analysis.

Jesus reported his giving analysis, too. Calling his disciples to him, Jesus said, "I tell you the truth, this poor widow has put more into the treasury than all the others" (Mk. 12:43b, NIV). Now, that's a "mitey" strange giving analysis, if you ask me. She gave less than everybody else. In fact, you couldn't buy a cup of coffee with her gift. The only way it could have been smaller would have been for her to keep one of those miserable little mites for herself. By what standard of measure can you possibly say that she gave more than all the others?

Jesus says, "They all gave out of their wealth; but she out of her poverty, put in everything—all she had to live on" (14:44, NIV). Jesus noticed some things that I missed in my analysis. You see, with my giving analysis, you are noticed according to *how much you give*. Jesus takes a different approach here with his giving analysis. Sometimes you don't measure a gift by what you give; you measure it by *what you keep* for yourself. The widow in our story won that one hands down.

I missed something else in my analysis because God reserves it for himself. It seems to me that God takes note of what we bring in our hearts before he honors what we bring in our hands. We've been talking about giving, but giving is a sign; it isn't the issue. The issue is what it means to be a disciple; that's why Jesus calls his disciples over at the beginning of this passage. He wants to make sure we don't miss the point. In verses 30 and 31, Jesus says that being a disciple is all about loving God and loving your neighbor. Then, in verses 38–40 he says (in essence), "You had better watch out for these teachers of the law. They look religious, but what they really love is to be noticed and praised by people. They say fancy prayers for people to hear, but they devour defenseless widows who barely have two *lepta* to rub together."

The giving is a sign. Jesus knows there is a kind of giving, however useful it might be, that doesn't have anything to do with love for God. But another kind of giving expresses a sold-out faith and love toward God and will hold nothing back from him. This widow did the very thing that the rich young man couldn't bring himself to do in Mark 10. She gave more than all the others because she did not consider her two little *lepta* things to be grasped, but she emptied herself in faithful obedience to God. Therefore, the Son of God exalted her. He noticed her. He turned the spotlight on her, and he said, "*This* is what I have been talking about." His disciples had only recently been arguing among themselves about who was the greatest. Now Jesus gets their attention and says, "Look at her. This is what discipleship is all about."

Giving analysis is a "mitey" strange business. It tells me some things, but it doesn't tell me everything, because some things are known only to God and to each of us as individuals before him. Sometimes a large gift is an act of faith and an expression of love and gratitude, but sometimes it is nothing more than a "tip" that will never be missed by the person who has great wealth. For some folks, a very small amount of giving may be a sign of selfishness and a lack of devotion. For others, that small gift represents a great sacrifice and is received and enjoyed as a pleasing aroma to the Lord.

Since we're on the subject of giving, let's spend just a few minutes talking about the bottom line. I think it may help us to be aware that in a culture like ours, we will always have to wrestle with the subject of money and giving. We live in the wealthiest nation on the face of this earth, and God has blessed almost all of us with more than enough to meet our basic needs. How much should I give? How much is it okay to keep for myself? How do I define and understand generosity? Do I know anything at all about sacrificial giving? Those are the kinds of questions that I have to struggle with when I understand the "Jesus style" of giving analysis. I hope you will wrestle with them, too, not for the purpose of generating guilt, but for the purpose of presenting ourselves and our money before God so that he can show us what he wants us to do. There won't be one set answer for all of us, but I believe God will lead each of us in this area if we will let him.

I want to close by having each of us ask ourselves one more question, because I believe it gets to the heart of what Jesus is teaching in this passage. What does my giving reveal about my understanding of discipleship? A few of you have asked specific questions about levels of giving. I don't want to get too far into that because easy answers and rules relieve us from the responsibility to wrestle with these questions, and I believe the Lord wants us to wrestle. Without making hard and fast rules, I will respond to a couple of concerns. Even after I notice the sharp difference between Jesus' giving analysis and the one I did a couple of weeks ago, I continue to be troubled by the large number who give nothing to the general fund. You can read through the history of God's people in both testaments of scripture, and what you will find is the recognition that it is unthinkable to come empty-handed to worship God. God's people have always offered their gifts to him, not because he needs them, but as a sign. Their gifts are a sign that they recognize that every blessing they have comes from God. Our gifts are a sign of allegiance and devotion to him. That's why you see the Old Testament concept of giving God the first fruits from the crop or the herd. The people understood that they were to give God the first and the best of what they had. If this is your church home, I hope you are receiving what God has for you here. He wants you to enjoy Christian fellowship, to be inspired by our worship together, to be fed from his Word, and to find opportunities to serve. He also wants you to learn how to give of your money. In doing so, you will learn to honor him with your finances, and you will live up to one of your commitments as a member of the family here. I can't think of any reason why it would be appropriate to be a member of a church and to do nothing to support the church financially.

Someone else mentioned that if tithing is the standard, and you don't feel like you can do that, discouragement sets in and you just say, "Why bother?" Then, you just don't give anything because you think it doesn't matter. Let me encourage you to forget about tithing for the moment and forget about how your giving does or doesn't impact the budget. Just start where you are. Make a commitment to regular, disciplined giving as an expression of your commitment to the Lord. Then, see where the Lord leads you. Don't give in to discouragement. Determine to trust God with your money, and I believe he will bless you and shape your attitude toward giving and money in a way that honors him. At the same time, I hope some of you will not hear that as an opportunity to be casual in your attitude toward giving. I'm not trying to make tithing a law, but I can't remember an instance in scripture in which God took favorable notice of someone's giving when they were giving less than a tithe. I really believe that God wants us to move past the tithe on our way to generosity, but we have to get *to* the tithe before we can get *past* it. Start where you can, and keep pursuing God's purpose for you in this area.

I really feel like I slighted one group when I did my analysis a couple of weeks ago, because you can't identify them by looking at numbers on a page. I can't even identify them now, but I have to believe some of you are here today. Some of you here today gave small dollar amounts to the general fund last year, but when you gave, it was the best you could do. It was an expression of sacrifice and commitment before the Lord. Some of us get strapped financially because we like to buy things; I'm not talking about us. I'm talking about those who are strapped by the circumstances of life— the loss of a job, or a divorce, or suffocating medical bills. Some of you are strapped in that way, but you are giving money to the Lord just as a way to express your faith in his promise to provide for you when you trust him. If I lumped you together with those of us who tend to be selfish with our money, I apologize. I just want to remind you again that the Lord sees things the rest of us can't see when those baskets go around each week.

I need to make my own personal confession, too. When I first looked at our giving analysis, I found where my family fit in. I was both surprised and a little bit proud. I could tell by the size of our gifts that we were doing our part. It was easy to compare myself with others and to point out their shortcomings. Perhaps I wouldn't have fared so well if I had compared what I kept for myself with others or if I had noticed the condition of my heart each Sunday when I gave. I didn't consider those things at all when I did my analysis, but that's what Jesus noticed. This discipleship is strange business. We have responded to the call to follow One who sends away a rich young man who could do so much for so many ministries, and who notices and praises a widow whose gift wouldn't buy a box of pencils.

Since Jesus made such a fuss over her, I thought I would just ask her what her secret was. She said:

> It's no secret. You people have a lot of money that you are worried about spending and managing. You give to budgets. You give "to support the work of the church." You

give when you are happy with the church leaders, and you don't give when you are unhappy with them. You give to this need or to that need, maybe even to help poor widows like me. I gave to the Lord! God is my refuge and strength. He is a defender of widows. Do you think I could take care of myself with those *lepta*? I put my trust in God. He can feed his children with manna from heaven, so why would I feel desperate or selfish? What's this game your young people play? Texas Hold 'Em? As they would say, "I'm all in."

I said, "I can see that, and I'm starting to understand why Jesus noticed you. You are pretty impressive, but I have to tell you that it's scary to think about following your lead. I want to be a good giver, but I like my 'stuff,' too."

She said, "Yes, it does simplify things when you don't have any 'stuff.' But the call to discipleship is the same for all of us. You remember what the Master said, 'Love the Lord your God with all your heart, and with all your soul, and with all your mind, and with all your strength. And love your neighbor as yourself.' If you can start to get a handle on that, maybe this whole business of giving and budgets will look different to you."

I know she's right. I can quote those great commands: Love the Lord your God with all your heart, and with all your soul, and with all your mind, and with all your strength; and love your neighbor as yourself. I know that's more important than all my giving and all my preaching and all the rest. I've still got my own wrestling to do with these things, and I'm guessing you do, too.

17

And They Crucified Him

Mark 15:21–41

DAVID KELLER

Compositional Comments

As an elder at the Grand Central Church of Christ in Vienna, West Virginia, I am occasionally called upon to fill the pulpit. When there is no pressing congregational need to address and when the sermon will stand isolated from the preaching context created by the full-time pulpit minister, I purposefully select a text or topic that is foundational to our Christian walk. For a recent preaching opportunity at Grand Central, I chose to look at the crucifixion of Jesus.

In preparation, I reexamined Morna Hooker's warning not to distort the meaning of the crucifixion in Mark by treating it in isolation from the resurrection. In her essay on the ending of Mark, she notes that Jesus presents the two as opposing sides of one coin in his passion predictions. Hooker notes how Mark ingeniously links the crucifixion and resurrection through the presence of the women in Jesus' ministry prior to the passion, during it, and at the site of the tomb. Hooker suggests that Mark's understated manner of presenting the resurrection might be paralleled by a similarly understated account of the crucifixion.

John Barton echoes Hooker's article in his reflections on Mark's account of the passion in relation to Mel Gibson's movie. Barton

169

addresses the temptation for all of us to create a Jesus in our own image and to suit our own purposes. I believe that one antidote to such distortion is balancing the tension between the meaning of any individual text and its relationship to the whole biblical narrative. In Mark 15:21–41, the text for this sermon, the crucifixion is both singular event *and* underlying current of all scripture. The passion relates the focal point of the history to which God has been leading his creation and from which he will direct its future. With Gibson and Barton, I wanted to understand "how he [Jesus] died" (15:39, NIV), what it was about his death that elicited the testimony of the centurion, "Surely, this man was the Son of God." I wanted to come to the text with the openness of a new hearer or reader. I wanted to mute the voices of those historical and theological preconceptions that the congregation and I already possess.

In this type of hearing and crafting, I'm following the wisdom of Fred Craddock's inductive method of rediscovering the story and then sharing that process of discovery in the sermon. Craddock's work encouraged me to respect Mark's narrative genius. I allow Mark's style and his message to be visible and make transparent my reflections on the text. As I examined Mark's style, I wrestled with the meaning of what he chose not to say. Specifically, I asked the questions of why Mark reveals so little about the physical suffering of Jesus, the immanence of God's will, and victory over death.

The Sermon: And They Crucified Him

The gospel accounts of Jesus' crucifixion tell an old, familiar story. Perhaps they're so familiar, it's hard to hear them any more. Mark's account may be the hardest to hear. His action-packed narrative, terse sentences, and Hemingway-like understatement may get our adrenaline flowing, but they also present a challenge. Mark rarely interprets events for us. He just describes them and immediately moves on. To find meaning, *we* have to work. Mark makes *us* think. And there may be no more thought-provoking text than his rendering of the crucifixion.

As we listen to Mark's account of Jesus' death, we know that we're at the climax of his gospel. If Mark is the superb storyteller that we suspect he is, we should be able to recognize that this is where the story has been heading right from the "get go." Mark begins the gospel with announcement of "good news," but if this story is going to grab us, such early pronouncements must actually warn of trouble ahead. In great stories, early good news is usually too good to be true. Sure enough, the gospel propels us to the crucifixion right from its opening scenes, beginning with Jesus' baptism, a sign to him and us of the sacrifice to come (10:38). When he begins his ministry, Jesus draws not only large crowds, but also violent opposition (2:1—3:6). Quickly, his enemies begin to look for ways to seek his life (3:6). When Jesus repeatedly predicts his own death and resurrection (8:31ff), the tension rises. As the conflict intensifies, we wonder how the story will play out. Who will triumph, Jesus or his opponents? Will the disciples catch on to the message in time? We are hoping by the time we conclude the narrative that the knot will begin to be untied and the mystery solved. In the suspense novels, at least, that's what's supposed to happen. So we listen to the story of the crucifixion. What is it that we hear?

Mark portrays a vivid landscape. Were we artists, we could render it in oil. Picture it in your imagination. We could place in the background in linear perspective the road on which Simon of Cyrene saunters into view on his way into Jerusalem for the Passover. With the right brush stroke we could catch the expression on his face as he is charged at spear point to pick up Jesus' cross and carry it. A large portion of the foreground will be filled with a retinue of Roman soldiers, guiding the procession, carrying tools of execution in lieu of weapons of war. A little higher on the canvas, just off center, we could shade in a hillock that even foreigners would easily recognize as "the place of the skull." We could sketch clusters of bystanders on the roadway, taking advantage of their proximity to this spectacle to belittle Jesus. Just off on one side, safely out of range of ceremonial contamination, we could gather the scribes and teachers of the law in their holy finery, out of earshot, enjoying their moment of victory, mocking Jesus in self-congratulation. On the other side of the canvas, barely visible, so distant that their expressions would be imperceptible, we would lightly touch in the women watching, just watching. The stage is dramatically set.

But something is missing. Where is the foreshadowing of triumph? How is this death going to yield victory? Where's the link to the resurrection Jesus predicted? Our favorite parts of this old, old story are missing. There is no incredible promise, "Today you will be with me in Paradise," to a penitent thief. No words of divine forgiveness, "Father, forgive them for they do not know what they do." No words of care and blessing upon a disciple and a mother. No "mission accomplished." Yes, the centurion senses something significant enough about Jesus' death to utter a startling confession, "Truly this man was God's Son." But what was it in "how Jesus died" that elicits this confession? Yes, there is the joy of a resurrection to come. But that, too, is so muted we're troubled. The first witnesses to the empty tomb see a young man, not Jesus, and then they flee in fear and disobedience. Something happens in this death that warranted victory. What? We want to know what Jesus does to win this spiritual war.

Mark demands that we look again. Now we see a glimpse, not of what Jesus does, but what he refuses to do. We see Jesus deny himself an anesthetic wine mingled with myrrh. Mark wants us to listen. What do we hear? An enigmatic cry, "My God, my God, why have you forsaken me?" But what have we heard? Is Jesus, like the psalmist he echoes, affirming in the face of adversity a faith rooted in God's loyalty to Israel? Or is it a statement of total abandonment and despair? Please, Mark, tell us! Tell us how to understand it all! Tell us what to believe! All we see is death.

But perhaps that's just the point. Perhaps Mark wants us to remember that crucifixion is about death, just death. Now, I know that statement sounds simplistic and obvious, but isn't it true that we rush to get beyond death? We don't like death. We don't want to deal with it. Our culture does back flips trying to deny its reality. We want to get beyond it as quickly as we can. We're hardwired to grieve, but grief is so painful, we escape to words of hope and encouragement before we allow ourselves to feel loss and emptiness. We have an eternal hope, but death must be reckoned with.

We want to get past the death of Jesus, too. We want to get the body off the cross, out of the grave, back into some recognizably divine form. Mark demands we see Jesus as fully human as well as fully divine. Jesus died. And his death was real. He was not a Gnostic ghost. A victory would come, but death came first. After the crucifixion, no one, not even the disciples, expected a victory. They just saw death. On our side of the empty tomb, maybe it's too easy for us to see that time in the grave as inconsequential. It wasn't inconsequential to Mary, his mother. It wasn't inconsequential to Mary Magdalene, nor to any of the disciples. Death is certainly not inconsequential when a loved one of ours dies.

While we're impressed by the power of Matthew's insistence of the fulfillment of prophecy in the passion week of Jesus, or by Luke's hint of triumph in Jesus' promise of paradise to the penitent thief, or by John's portrayal of Jesus' unity with the Father, for us,

Mark clears the deck. It is the death of Jesus that counts. This atoning sacrifice, the ransom for sin, is what Jesus said he came to do: "For the Son of Man came not to be served but to serve, and to give his life [as] a ransom for many" (10:45). When Jesus said that one must lose one's life to save it, he was talking about himself as well as the disciples. Mark's spare, unadorned prose makes the central message unmistakable. "And they crucified him." The crowds came and went. The disciples left. The women stood far off. Few people may have actually witnessed the moment of Jesus' death. But Mark puts us there, right next to the centurion. We look with his eyes, those eyes that had the responsibility to see that the deed was done, those eyes that could not turn away from the gruesomeness and obscenity, those eyes that saw a man die and in that death saw "the Son of God."

So, what do we do with this death? If we accept that Jesus died, how are we to respond to it? I don't think it's as much a matter of what we are to do as much as what we should allow the death to do to us. When was the last time you were moved, moved deeply and emotionally, while participating in the Lord's supper? Don't we all wish that we could reclaim some long lost spiritual fire in our lives? Perhaps being willing to look at death, as hard as it is and as little as we want to do it, will allow God to open our hearts to rekindle that fire. Perhaps we can take a clue from Peter, who proclaims the power to "live your lives as strangers," as God's people in a fallen world. The power is in remembering we have been redeemed, "not with perishable things such as silver and gold," but "with the precious blood of Christ" (1 Peter 1:17–19, NIV).

When we think of the death of Jesus, Mark forces us to observe something unusual. If we're to remember the death of Jesus, we expect that it's the physical suffering that we're to respond to. But when we look back at Mark's painting, we have another problem. We can paint much of the picture, but what are we to do with the most important element in the picture? How do we paint Jesus? When we look to Mark to guide our brush stroke, all we hear is, "And they crucified him…And they crucified him." It's almost as if Mark wants us behind the cross, not able to see what happens when someone is crucified.

What Mel Gibson took such pains to portray—the horrific suffering of Jesus, Mark is hesitant to show. We don't see the nails through the wrists or in the feet. We don't see the crown of thorns pressed down puncturing the brow. We don't see the bloody

wounds, some dried and clotted, some still flowing freely. We don't
see his pierced side or the gashes on his legs and back. Mark turns
us away from the torturous details. I know a man who, when he
viewed Gibson's film, didn't see the details either. He couldn't
watch for a while. He had to turn his face. He wanted to look, but
couldn't. He knew enough about what he would see that he turned
away. I suspect he was not alone.

I doubt Mark wants to minimize the suffering of Jesus, but he
clearly wants to print in bold type the *temptation* for Jesus to give
up on his mission, to deny his identity, literally to leave the cross.
If the suffering had significance, it would be in the temptation for
Jesus to deny God's will and reject the cross as the way to glory.
The details of Mark's text suggest that Jesus was surrounded and
tempted by avenues of escape. The appearance of Simon of Cyrene
proclaims that someone else should be bearing this burden, sinners
like Simon, or like me, or like you. The placard above Jesus' head,
reading "The King of the Jews," would remind him of his true
identity and further tempt Jesus to call down those twelve legions
of angels to deliver him. The passersby call for him to come down
from the cross. The chief priests call for him to come down from
the cross. The teachers of the law call for him to come down from
the cross. Those who misunderstand Jesus' Aramaic "My God, my
God" believe he's calling for Elijah. They try to sustain his life with
fluids to see if Elijah will come to bring Jesus down from the cross.
"Come down from the cross" is the refrain of this hymn.

Mark asks us to see the crucifixion of Jesus as a temptation to
flee from his destiny. We, too, are called upon to persevere, to remain
faithful despite the trials and temptations we bear. For the
Corinthians, Paul used the victory of the resurrection as the basis
of encouraging these Christians to stay their course, to stand firm,
not be moved (15:58). Mark, however, gives us Jesus and the cross
and tells us to stay the course despite the potential for abandonment, suffering, and abuse. Our cross may not be a literal one, but
our world calls us to come down from our crosses every day. Come
down from your cross. Come down. The message of Mark, the
message of the cross, is to persevere. Stand firm; stay the course.
That's the way to victory.

Finishing the Story We Find Ourselves In

Mark 16:1–8

ROBERT STEPHEN REID

Compositional Comments

Fred Craddock sets the tone in this volume by preaching a 70 C.E. rather than a 30 C.E. Jesus. In other words, he focuses on how Mark shaped the story of Jesus for a particular community of disciples who are already believing Christians. Preaching a 70 C.E. Jesus lets the preacher tell the story of Jesus, but also tells the story of how the gospel writer is using the story to call forth faith from listeners and readers. Since I am not an accomplished Southern storyteller, I have adopted a different voice than Craddock. However, at least one of my illustrations is offered as an *homage* to Craddock's wonderful self-effacing style of creating moments of listener identification.

From Morna Hooker, I have drawn the concern to work on the play of ideas involved in what counts as evidence between "seeing is believing vs. believing is seeing." She argues that Mark's abrupt ending forces its recipients to go back into the gospel story to find its meaning and there find the evidence for belief. In this sermon I push the limits of her believing/seeing interplay in my own reflection on the function of Mark's ending.

I set the sermon in the context of an Easter service since this would be the typical occasion for preaching this text. With a nod to the performance theory that shapes so much of Richard Ward's work in chapter 7, I seek to invite my listeners to become learners who go and do the performative claim of the text. Since I believe that Mark's disturbing ending is intentional, my task is to perform an intention aligned with its purpose for respondents today.[1] To this end I employ a Ricoeurian sermon design that invites listeners to move "From First Naiveté to Second Naiveté."[2] The title of the sermon is a variation of the title of a novel by Brian McLaren.[3]

The Sermon: Finishing the Story We Find Ourselves in

Here we are gathered on this triumphant day to join with the chorus of Christians across two millennia. And though I know you have already said it, let me give you the opportunity again:

PREACHER: "Christ is risen!"
PEOPLE: **"He is risen, indeed!"**

Historically, this ancient Easter affirmation of the church is called *Christos Anesti*—Christ is risen. It comes from the gospel of Mark, in this text in which the women find a young man, dressed all in white, who tells them, "He is risen!" Only in Mark's gospel is this affirmation, "He is risen!" a stand-alone phrase. In the second century the church simply replaced the pronoun with the title "Christ." And now we have, "Christ is risen!" "He is risen, indeed!"[4] This has been the testimony of the Christian community down through the ages, claimed and counterclaimed, every Easter morning anew. We believe in the resurrection.

Every year, lectors in our congregations around the world step front and center, assume the role of Mark's young man in the tomb, and proclaim: "Christ is risen!" And we, like every generation come before us, respond by *rewriting the end* of Mark's gospel. Unlike the women who flee from the tomb in terror and amazement, who say "nothing to anyone, for they were afraid," we make the story end well. We, in joyous reply, respond: "He is risen, indeed!" We say what we believe.

And so every Easter since the story was first told, Christians have gathered anew to amend the conclusion of Mark's gospel. What was he thinking, ending it like that? Alarm. Terror. Amazement. Fear. And finally, awkward silence. What kind of writer would stop there?

The episode starts well; or seems to. We have women—Mary Magdalene, Mary the mother of James, and a woman called Salome—taking spices in hand on their way to the tomb for the final burial arrangements left unfinished in the rush to get his body in the ground before Sabbath. These are faithful women, the ones still willing to risk everything even though the "faithful" men have fled from Jesus' side. So here are the women on their way to the tomb, when Mark decides to tell us that they were asking one another, "Who will roll away the stone for us from the entrance to the tomb?" Of all the words he could have reported to us about their conversation on the way, why this? It's not a very flattering picture, is it? These poor women, who are just trying to do the right thing, the faithful thing, are presented as well-meaning airheads who forgot to bring along the most important thing of all—some men to help move the stone.

When I am on my way to a conference, my wife Barbara is helpful to the point of being *almost* bothersome.

"Do you have your presentation notes?" she asks.

"Right there," I say, pointing to my briefcase.

"Do you have your hotel reservation receipt?"

"Right here with my flight tickets," I say, patting my leather travel holder.

"Did you pack the wireless receiver for the laptop?"

"Right in the computer carrier side pocket. I packed the power cord, too," I add.

"Did you remember to bring some of your business cards?"

"Oh. That's a good idea. I forgot."

We all know how frustrating it is to get somewhere only to realize we forgot to bring things we really need. Yet Mark reports that these women realize what they forgot on the way and then they just keep going. If this is a set-up for their eyewitness testimony a jury will hear later, it does not present them in the best light. Add this to their running away and the fact that their defense counsel admits that they remained silent when they should have told people what they saw, and—well—any prosecutor would find it fairly easy to discredit their testimony. Let's be honest here. Some Bible critics have noticed this. Perhaps the women had asked men to accompany them. Maybe the men had refused. Mark simply does not tell us. All we are told is that these women are on their way to do something very important and are admitting that, by all rights, the whole trip is pointless without some men to help.

But they keep going.

More than any other portion of Mark's story of Jesus, we become acutely aware of Mark's own voice in this last episode. Of course, at other moments along the way his voice surfaces. Once he interrupts Jesus' teaching about the difference between ritual purity and true purity of heart with a parenthetical explanation of Jewish ritual hand washing (7:3–4). Another time, after a story about Jesus telling his followers, "Whoever wishes to become great among you must be your servant," Mark adds his own commentary that, "The Son of Man came not to be served but to serve, and to give his life a ransom for many" (10:45). And yet another time he interrupts Jesus' prophecy about a "desolating sacrilege" being set up in the temple with the words, "Let the reader understand" (13:14). In other words, we have heard from Mark the writer already along the way. But this last episode is different. At the end of this gospel his voice becomes very apparent in a disturbing way. Suddenly we find ourselves questioning his judgment as a writer. And why not? Everyone else down through history seems to question the wisdom of this abrupt ending.

Aside from the way we believers have amended it every Easter with our *Christos Anesti*, others have also felt the need to change Mark's ending, too. Most of our Bibles contain these extra endings written by other people. A short one says that the women did go and tell Peter what they saw and that a resurrected Jesus gave followers further instructions. A longer one provides lots of accounts of the witnesses to the resurrection of Jesus—the kind of testimony that generally holds up better in a court of law. On top of this, we also have Matthew, Luke, and John, who all decided that they could make a better run at telling the story of Jesus, and so wrote gospels that fix the ending, too. Everyone seems to think that the story isn't complete unless we hear the evidence that many people saw Jesus after he rose from the grave.[5] After all, when it comes to proof, "seeing is believing." And on Easter we are accustomed to hearing the stories about people who believed because they saw Jesus, right?

Isn't that how John's gospel ends with Thomas, the famous doubter, who finally sees Jesus and believes? Remember Thomas? When Jesus said that he was going back to Bethany because Lazarus was dead, Thomas turned aside to the rest of the followers, rolled his eyes, and said, "Sure, let's go too. Maybe we can die with him" (Jn. 11:16 paraphrased). This Thomas never wanted to come to Jerusalem in the first place, and now is anxious to get out of town. So, when Jesus said he was going away and that they knew the way to the place he was going, this ever hopeful Thomas says, "Wait a minute Lord, we don't know where you are going. How do you expect us to rendezvous with you unless you tell us?"(14:5 paraphrased).[6] Then the worst happens. Jesus is captured and crucified. Everyone else hides away in fear, but not Thomas. As far as he is concerned, it's finished. All his hopes and dreams are shattered because Jesus wouldn't be reasonable. So when the others tell him they have *seen* the risen Jesus, this is the Thomas we know. He says, "I won't believe unless I see with my own eyes. As far as I am concerned, seeing is believing"(20:25 paraphrased).[7] And that's how John's gospel sets up the end. Thomas sees the risen Lord and believes. "Seeing is believing." John's gospel ends with the most pragmatic of the disciples making the greatest leap of faith. He doesn't just admit that Jesus must be the Lord because he is among them. He says, "My Lord and my God!" (20:28).[8] With this ultimate confession, John the evangelist ends his gospel with a final word of hope from Jesus on behalf of every generation that would come after. Jesus says to Thomas: "Have you believed because you have seen me? Blessed are those who have not seen and yet have come to believe" (20:29).[9] Now that is an ending. But here we are today with Mark's awkward ending. What have we got? Three women, the gospel's last best hope for people who might see the truth. And what do they do? Run for their lives and say nothing to anyone. More than any other moment, it is here that we become acutely aware of Mark's own voice as the writer of this final episode of his gospel.

Do you feel the same urge so many others have had to rewrite this ending? Imagine yourself as one of the first people who heard this gospel read. It's four-thirty in the morning. And you've gotten up early each day to hear more of this incredible account of your Lord and Master, Jesus. You have listened with awe to the stories of Jesus' teaching and his miracles. You have ached at the bumbling misunderstanding and misconceptions of his followers. You were horrified and heartbroken as you heard how one by one each of them fled as the end drew near. You wept bitter tears when you heard how Jesus died. You felt Jesus' heart-cry of God-forsakenness on the cross. He let them take his life that you might have a life that matters. But, this morning, the triumphant moment you have waited days for has come. The story of the empty tomb will be read. "Do not be alarmed," God's messenger says, "You are looking for Jesus of Nazareth, who was crucified. He has been raised; he is not here…[H]e is going ahead of you…" Your heart sings at hearing these words. Your whole life is wrapped up in this one hope: that God was, in Christ, redeeming your life so that your life will matter for God. But then the lector finishes the story and tells you that the women flee in fear. "They said nothing to anyone!"

Impossible! How can they be silent in the face of such wonder? And you, like many who will come after you, desperately want to fix the ending of this gospel. "If they cannot see the truth, I do," you say. "I believe. Let me go! Let me finish this story. Let me tell what happened."

Perhaps, just perhaps, Mark knew what he was doing. Perhaps it is no accident that this gospel ends desperately needing to be fixed, desperately needing a better ending. In the gospels of Matthew and Luke, "seeing is believing." They end with testimonies of witnesses to the resurrection. John ends his Gospel, not with Thomas' dictum, "seeing is believing," but with Jesus' telling future followers that for them, "believing is seeing." But could it be that for Mark the only testimony that matters is the witness of the believer who will act to fix the end of his gospel? Perhaps for Mark, "believing is…doing?" It would seem that for our gospel writer Mark, "Believing is nothing less than responding—our going, our telling, our doing?" Believing is fixing the ending of his story. More than just saying what we believe, Mark forces the hand of those who hear his gospel, challenging every generation to take up the task of following Jesus, of going and doing what we say we believe.

Once, at a conference, I tried to help people experience the narrative force of this abrupt ending by illustrating the effect with a limerick:[10]

An elephant went to Seattle
prepared to engage in a battle.
The rain doused his trunk,
which promptly shrunk…

I just left it like that. I never finished it for them. When the hour was over, I was ready to field questions. Of course, I wanted to talk about what Mark had written, but many of the people who came forward just wanted to hear the last line of the limerick.

"It doesn't have a last line," I said. Not to be deterred, people took that as an invitation to devise a best ending. You would think I had created a contest. It became the talk of the conference. In fact, even as I speak, some of you are mentally trying to devise a satisfying ending for it. Our stake in limerick resolution is that strong. Imagine if our stake in gospel resolution was equally as strong? Imagine what could happen if believing is more than seeing. Imagine if it is *doing*?

A congregation struggles to come to terms with how to respond honorably to a longtime member who is soon to be paroled. He is a convicted child molester who has repeatedly confessed his sin to God and continues to ask for God's help to redeem the remainder of his life. The congregation leaders ask, "Can such a person really be redeemed?" He wants to come back to this congregation. The question is whether it is better for him to be where everyone knows and proper precautions can be set in place, or is it better to refuse, sending him out to another congregation where he will be anonymous? Can they risk becoming known in the community as the church that welcomes sex offenders? What if word got out? Would visitors even come to such a church? Join such a church? They respond. They begin to hold meetings with counseling professionals to determine what precautions must be put in place so that they can welcome home their brother who once was lost and now is found.

(With arms spread to invite the *Christos Anesti* response:)
"Christ is risen!"
(The congregation responds)
"He is risen, indeed!

A man commits his Saturdays to the local rescue mission breakfast. He doesn't volunteer to serve the meals, or sort the donated clothes. He simply shows up to eat. He gets in line and is served his food, finds a table, eats and talks and listens. He talks about politics and the news and listens. He talks about family and failures and listens. He talks about faith and doubt and listens. Saturday after Saturday he shows up, gets in line, gets his food, eats, talks and listens. He makes friends. When appropriate, he finds ways to help these friends. Sometimes he gets burned in the process. But he continues to respond; he keeps showing up.

(With arms spread to invite the *Christos Anesti* response:)
"Christ is risen!"
(The congregation responds)
"He is risen, indeed!"

So let's *go* and keep finishing this story we find ourselves in where *doing* is *believing*. And the Easter promise is that Jesus will *go* before us. Amen.

Notes

Introduction

[1]The dissolution of old barriers and reformation of new alliances is prevalent in the current Emergent Movement (recently birthed from the Evangelicals) and the Missional church (developed within the Protestant Mainline).

[2]Craddock quibbles in the pages of this book with the movement's designation and his impact.

[3]Matthew 21:12–22. Matthew's arrangement moves simply from temple cleansing (vv. 12–17) to the fig tree's being cursed and withering (vv. 18–20) to teaching (vv. 21–22).

[4]Mark 11:12–26.

[5]Fred B. Craddock, *Preaching* (Nashville: Abingdon Press, 1986), 161.

[6]Ibid., 162.

[7]See Robert S. Reid, "Exploring Preaching's Voice from Ex Cathedra to Exilic," in *Preaching the Eighth Century Prophets,* ed. David Fleer and Dave Bland (Abilene, Tex.: Abilene Christian University Press, 2004), 135–64.

[8]This is Maya Angelou's comment to Craddock, from Fred Craddock, "Reflections for the Next Generation," Sermon Seminar, Rochester College, May 25, 2005.

[9]See Morna D. Hooker, *Beginnings: Keys that Open the Gospels* (London: SCM, 1997) and Morna D. Hooker, *Endings: Invitations to Discipleship* (Peabody, Mass.: Hendrickson, 2003).

[10]Craddock, "Reflections for the Next Generation."

Chapter 1: Jesus Deeply Grieved

[1]This chapter maintains the oral quality of Fred Craddock's sermon delivered at Rochester College in May, 2005.

[2]Not so called in John.

Chapter 2: The New Homiletic for Latecomers

[1]This chapter maintains the oral quality of Fred Craddock's presentation delivered at Rochester College, May 2005.

[2]Morna Hooker said this in a delightful way. See in this volume her essay "This Is the Good News,"especially 33–34.

[3]See in this volume "Jesus Deeply Grieved," especially 8–9.

[4]See C. Clifton Black, "The Education of Human Wanting: Formation by *Pater Noster,*" in *Character & Scripture: Moral Formation, Community, and Biblical Interpretation*, ed. William Brown (Grand Rapids: Eerdmans, 2002), 248–63.

Chapter 3: This Is the Good News

[1]Morna D. Hooker, *Beginnings: Keys that Open the Gospels* (London: SCM, 1997; Harrisburg, Pa.: TPI, 1998).

[2]E.g., L. E. Keck, "The Introduction to Mark's Gospel," *NTS* 12 (1996): 352–70.

[3]I have discussed Mark's use of Isaiah in Morna D. Hooker, "The Way of the Lord: Isaiah in St. Mark's Gospel," in *BJRL* (2005).

[4]Isaiah 29:13. The form of the text is closer to the LXX than to the Hebrew.

[5]Note the way in which the story of the temple (11:11, 15–19) is interwoven with that of the fig tree (11:12–14, 20–24). See also Mark 13:1–2.

[6]Mark 12:10. Cf. 14:58; although the accusation that Jesus threatened to destroy the temple is described as false testimony, Mark suggests that it is a *distortion* of the

truth, for in 13:1–2 Jesus is said to have prophesied its destruction; similarly, the reference to "three days" in 14:58 suggests that Mark intends us to think of God raising Jesus from the dead. Like John (2:13–22) and Paul (1 Cor. 2:10–17), Mark appears to be thinking of the Christian community as "the new temple."

[7]See Matthew 11:10; Luke 7:27.

[8]On the use of prophetic signs, see W. D. Stacey, *Prophetic Drama in the Old Testament* (London: Epworth, 1990). I have explored the use of prophetic signs by Jesus and by John in Morna D. Hooker, *The Signs of a Prophet* (London: SCM/ Harrisburg, Pa.: TPI, 1997) and Morna D. Hooker, "John's Baptism: A Prophetic Sign," in *The Holy Spirit and Christian Origins: Essays in Honor of James D. G. Dunn*, ed. Graham N. Stanton, Bruce W. Longenecker, and Stephen C. Barton (Grand Rapids: Eerdmans, 2004), 22–40.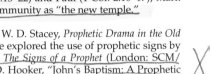

[9]E.g., Jeremiah 4:14; Ezekiel 36:25; Psalm 51:7.

[10]Genesis 6:17; Jeremiah 47:2–4; Psalm 106:11.

[11]Isaiah 35:6–7; 44:3–4; Ezekiel 17:5–6; 47:1–12.

[12]Isaiah 4:4. Cf. Isaiah 30:28; Jeremiah 4:11. "Spirit," "breath," and "wind" are all translations of the Hebrew word *ruaḥ*.

[13]Mark 1:10; 3:28–30.

[14]I have discussed this more fully in Hooker, "John's Baptism."

[15]The Hebrew word, "*elohim*," literally "gods," is the term used for God. The LXX, the Greek translation of the Old Testament, understood it here to mean "angels."

[16]Cf. Morna D. Hooker, *The Son of Man in Mark* (London: SPCK/Montreal: McGill, 1967).

Chapter 4: Believe and Follow

[1]Morna D. Hooker, *Endings: Invitations to Discipleship* (London: SCM/Peabody, Mass.: Hendrickson, 2003).

[2]Mark 8:31; 9:31; 10:33.

[3]Mark 9:9–13 follows the transfiguration; 10:45 is part of Jesus' response to the request of James and John in 10:35–37. Promises of vindication in 13:26–27 and 14:62 are the triumphant response to imminent suffering.

[4]Mark 8:34–38; 10:38–39.

[5]1 Corinthians 1:10–31; 4:6–16. Cf. Romans 6.

[6]This lack of understanding is underlined by Mark in 9:6.

[7]1 Kings 1:32–40. Gihon is a spring in Jerusalem.

[8]E.g., Mark 12:6, 35–37.

[9]Mark 13:6, 21, 26, 32.

[10]For this suggestion, see David Catchpole, *Resurrection People: Studies in the Resurrection Narratives of the Gospels* (London: Darton, Longman, and Todd, 2000), 52.

Chapter 5: Mark and Becoming Fully Human

[1]Wayne Booth, *The Company We Keep: An Ethics of Fiction* (Berkeley: University of California Press, 1988), 229, argues that in reading literature, "a first step is to reconsider our notions about the formation of 'character'—of self, of soul, of ethos, of personality, of identity. How do our current conceptions of who we are and how we develop differ from those of earlier periods?" In this essay, I ask a similar question of the gospel of Mark.

[2]See Stanley Cavell, *Cities of Words: Pedagogical Letters on a Register of the Moral Life* (Cambridge, Mass.: Harvard University Press, 2004). Martha Nussbaum, *Love's Knowledge* (New York: Oxford University Press, 1990), 24f., adds: "No starting point is altogether neutral here. No way of putting the search, putting the question, fails to contain some hint as to where the answers might lie. Questions set things up in one way or another, tell us what to include, what to look for."

[3]Michael Walzer, *Thick and Thin: Moral Argument at Home and Abroad* (Notre Dame, Ind.: University of Notre Dame Press, 1997), 98.

[4]Charles Taylor, *Sources of the Self* (Cambridge, Mass.: Harvard University Press, 1989), 27.

[5]See Frederick D. Aquino, *Communities of Informed Judgment: Newman's Illative Sense and Accounts of Rationality* (Washington, D.C.: Catholic University of America Press, 2004).

[6]Cavell, *Cities of Words*, 16.

[7]Paul Ricoeur, "Naming God," *Union Seminary Quarterly Review* 24 (1979): 219.

[8]David Rhoads, *Reading Mark, Engaging the Gospel* (Minneapolis: Fortress Press, 2004), 12.

[9]J. P. Heil, "Reader-Response and the Narrative Context of the Parables about Growing Seed in Mark 4:1–34," *Catholic Biblical Quarterly* 54 (1992): 285.

[10]Ibid., 275, points out that "Mark's implied audience identifies the 'sower' with Jesus who went out to preach the gospel of God with the announcement that 'the time is fulfilled and the kingdom of God is at hand! Repent and believe in the gospel!'"

[11]Kent Brower, "Mark 9:1: Seeing the Kingdom in Power," *Journal for the Study of the New Testament* 6 (1980): 39.

[12]Donald H. Juel, "The Origin of Mark's Christology," in *The Messiah: Developments in Earliest Judaism and Christianity*, ed. James H. Charlesworth (Minneapolis: Fortress Press, 1992), 453.

[13]Joel Marcus, "Mark 4:10–12 and Marcan Epistemology," *Journal of Biblical Literature* 103 (1984): 571, says that the centurion sees the cross differently than the other bystanders. "While others see without perceiving, to the centurion is granted the mystery of the kingdom of God." Brower, "Mark 9:1," 38, maintains that "the whole death scene in Mk 15:33–39 has distinct Day of the Lord features which make the designation apposite. The cosmic phenomena, presented in undoubted allusion to Am 8:9, suggest strongly that Mk viewed the crucifixion in this fashion. It is in the shameful death of Jesus that the readers can discern the judgment of mankind in general (v. 33), and Judaism in particular (v. 38). In the depth of weakness, the power of judgment occurs."

[14]Dorothy A. Lee-Pollard, "Powerlessness as Power: A Key Emphasis in the Gospel of Mark," *Scottish Journal of Theology* 40 (1992): 176.

[15]Dan O. Via, Jr., *The Ethics of Mark's Gospel—In the Middle of Time* (Philadelphia: Fortress Press, 1985), 131.

[16]Lee-Pollard, "Powerlessness as Power," 186.

[17]John D. Zizioulas, *Being as Communion: Studies in Personhood and the Church* (Crestwood, N.Y.: St. Vladimir's Seminary Press, 1993).

[18]Ibid., 94.

[19]Richard Moran, *Authority and Estrangement: An Essay on Self-Knowledge* (Princeton, N.J.: Princeton University Press, 2001), xxxiv. Moran does not tackle the question of selfhood in Mark, but his phenomenological focus is ripe for Markan appropriation.

Chapter 6: If Mark the Evangelist Could See Mel Gibson's *The Passion of the Christ*

[1]Unless otherwise indicated, all scriptural references in this essay will employ the *New International Version* of the Bible.

[2]Ludwig Wittgenstein, *Philosophical Investigations*, 3d ed., trans. G. E. M. Anscombe (Cambridge, Mass.: Blackwell, 2001), part 2, section 11, 166.

[3]On different perspectives on the film, see especially the articles by Jim Wallis, Susan Thistlethwaite, and Mary Boys in *Perspectives on* The Passion of the Christ: *Religious Thinkers and Writers Explore the Issues Raised by the Controversial Movie*, ed. Jonathan Burnham (New York: Miramax Books, 2004).

[4]John Dominic Crossan, "Hymn to a Savage God," in *Jesus and Mel Gibson's* The Passion of the Christ: *The Film, the Gospels and the Claims of History*, ed. Kathleen E. Corley and Robert L. Webb (London: Continuum, 2004), 8–27.

[5]This review appeared in March of 2004 and is also quoted in Susan Thistlethwaite, "Mel Makes a War Movie," in *Perspectives*, 135.

[6]See Jim Wallis, "*The Passion* and the Message," in *Perspectives*, 113–14.

[7]Thomas E. Wartenberg, "*Passion of the Christ*: Do Jews and Christians See the Same Film?" in *Mel Gibson's* Passion *and Philosophy: The Cross, the Questions, the Controversy*, ed. Jorge J. E Gracia (Chicago: Open Court, 2004), 83. For thoughtful articles on these issues, also see Amy-Jill Levine, "First Take the Log Out of Your Own Eye: Different Viewpoints, Different Movies," in *Perspectives*, 197–210; and Mark Goodacre, "The Power of *The Passion*: Reacting and Over-reacting to Gibson's Artistic Vision," in *Jesus and Mel Gibson's* The Passion, 28–44.

[8]See Eugene Korn and John Pawlikowski, "Commitment to Community: Interfaith Relations and Faithful Witness," in *Perspectives*, 182.

[9]Crossan, "Hymn to a Savage God," 8.

[10]David J. Goa, "*The Passion*, Classical Art and Re-presentation," in *Jesus and Mel Gibson's* The Passion, 152.

[11]Also see a number of insightful treatments of other characters from the film, such as Judas, Satan, Mary, other female characters, Pilate, and the Jewish leaders, in *Jesus and Mel Gibson's* The Passion.

[12]See Anne Catherine Emmerich, *The Dolorous Passion of Our Lord Jesus Christ* (El Sobrante, Calif.: North Bay Books, 2004).

[13]Quoted in Thistlethwaite, "Mel Makes a War Movie," 139.

[14]Stephen Prothero, "Jesus Nation, Catholic Christ," in *Perspectives*, 267–82. See also Ralph McInerny, "Who Do You Say That I Am," in *Mel Gibson's* Passion *and Philosophy*, 1–6.

[15]Frederick D. Aquino, chapter 5 of this book; Morna D. Hooker, chapter 4.

[16]Robert L. Webb and Kathleen E. Corley, "Introduction: *The Passion*, the Gospels and the Claims of History," in *Jesus and Mel Gibson's* The Passion, 3.

[17]Ibid.

[18]Ibid.

[19]Jon Meacham, "Who Really Killed Jesus?" in *Perspectives*, 13.

[20]Frederick Zugibe, *The Crucifixion of Jesus: A Forensic Inquiry*, 2d ed., rev. and exp. (New York: M. Evans and Company, 2005), 60–64.

[21]For a thoughtful discussion on this, see Ben Witherington III, "Numb Struck: An Evangelical Reflects on Gibson's *Passion*," in *Perspectives*, 81–94.

[22]Meacham, "Who Really Killed Jesus?" 3.

[23]Jay Tolson and Linda Kulman, "The Other Jesus: How a Jewish Reformer Lost His Jewish Identity," in *Perspectives*, 18.

[24]Mark 14:33, 34, 36, 50, 64, 65; 15:1, 15, 17, 19, 20.

[25]For more details, see Gareth B. Matthews, "The Death of Socrates and the Death of Christ," in *Mel Gibson's* Passion *and Philosophy*, 179–89.

[26]See David Keller, "And They Crucified Him," chapter 16 in this volume, 173.

[27]For a good presentation of different theories of atonement, for example, and their relationship to the film, see Jerry L. Walls, "Christ's Atonement: Washing Away Human Sin," in *Mel Gibson's* Passion *and Philosophy*, 25–39; and Robert K. Johnson, "*The Passion* as Dynamic Icon: A Theological Reflection," in *Re-Viewing the Passion: Mel Gibson's Film and Its Critics*, ed. S. Brent Plate (New York: Palgrave Macmillan, 2004), 55–70.

[28]Dallas Willard, *The Divine Conspiracy: Rediscovering Our Hidden Life in God* (New York: HarperCollins, 1997), 403, n. 8.

[29]James Martin, S.J., "The Last Station: A Catholic Reflection on *The Passion*," in *Perspectives*, 108–9.

[30]Mel Gibson, as quoted in Webb and Corley, "Introduction: *The Passion*," 2.

Chapter 7: The End Is Performance

[1]I am indebted to Professor David Rhoads for this term. He uses it in an unpublished manuscript, "Performance Criticism: A New Methodology in Biblical Studies?" (2004). Professor Thomas E. Boomershine and Adam Bartholomew use a related term for the same practice: "recital criticism."

[2]See Samuel Laeuchli, "The Expulsion from the Garden and the Hermeneutics of Play," in *The Body and the Bible: Interpreting and Experiencing Biblical Narratives*, ed. Bjorn Krondorfer (Philadelphia: Trinity International, 1992), 27.

[3]Walter J. Ong, S.J., "A Dialectic of Aural and Objective Correlatives," in *Critical Theory Since Plato*, ed. Hazard Adams (New York: Harcourt Brace Jovanovich, 1971), 1160, 1164.

[4]Alfred Corn, ed., *Incarnation: Contemporary Writers on the New Testament* (New York: Penguin Books, 1990), xii.

[5]Walter Wink, *The Bible in Human Transformation: Toward a New Paradigm for Biblical Study* (Philadelphia: Fortress Press, 1973).

[6]Pierre Babin, with Mercedes Iannone, *The New Era in Religious Communication*, trans. David Smith (Minneapolis: Augsburg Fortress Press, 1991), 14. "The manner of presentation is what gives life and form to the material words of Christ."

[7]Henry Jankiewicz, "Concepts of Rhetoric," http://web.syr.edu/~hjjankie/209/cncpts.rhet.html, p. 1.

[8]Patrick R. Keifert, "Mind Reader and Maestro: Models for Understanding Biblical Interpreters," *Word and World* 1:2 (Spring 1981): 157.

[9]Wolfgang Iser, *The Act of Reading: A Theory of Aesthetic Response* (Baltimore: Johns Hopkins University Press, 1978), 18.

[10]Carol Simpson Stern and Bruce Henderson, *Performance: Texts and Contexts* (New York and London: Longman, 1993), 263.

[11]Keifert, "Mind Reader and Maestro," 160.

[12]I am indebted here to the insights Nicholas Lash develops in *Theology on the Way to Emmaus* (London: SCM Press, 1986), 37–46.

[13]For essential insights on how this text may be spoken in a performed interpretation, see Morna Hooker's essay in chapter 4 of this volume.

[14]Serene Jones and Richard F. Ward, "Traumatic Unendings: Violence, Preaching, and the Gospel of Mark," unpublished manuscript, 17.

Chapter 9: A Window into the Kingdom

[1]Roy H. Williams, "Perceptual Reality," *Monday Morning Memo*, July 18, 2005. From *Touch Points* Web log, http://wizardofadscanada.typepad.com/touch_points/2005/07/mmm_for_july_18.html.

[2]John Shea, "The Indiscriminate Host," in *Stories of Faith* (Chicago: Thomas More Press, 1980), 180.

[3]Quoted by Steve Chalke, *The Lost Message of Jesus* (Grand Rapids: Zondervan, 2003), 165.

[4]Christnet is a roving shelter in which area churches house homeless persons for one week each.

Chapter 10: "Who Is Jesus?"

[1]"Master, the Tempest Is Raging," words by Mary A. Baker, 1874.

[2]Arnold M. Ludwig, *How Do We Know Who We Are? A Biography of the Self* (New York: Oxford, 1997), 101–20. Crane's biographer was Christopher Benfey, *The Double Life of Stephen Crane* (New York: Knopf, 1992).

Chapter 13: Only the Blind Can See

[1]See Mark 8; 9; and 10 for Jesus' three predictions and the disciples' inappropriate responses.

Chapter 14: Radical Discipleship

[1]"Great View, Less Sweat," *Newsweek* (June 28, 2004): 57.

[2]A story related by William Willimon in *Pulpit Resources* Logos Productions.

[3]Dallas Willard writes, "So far as the visible Christian institutions of our day are concerned, discipleship is clearly optional…Churches are filled with 'undiscipled disciples,' as Jess Moody has called them," in *The Spirit of the Disciplines—Reissue: Understanding How God Changes Lives* (New York: HarperCollins, 1991), 259.

[4]Lee Camp, *Mere Discipleship* (Grand Rapids, Mich.: Brazos Press, 2002), 96.

[5]William Willimon and Stanley Hauerwaus, *The Truth about God* (Nashville: Abingdon Press, 1999), 38.

Chapter 18: Finishing the Story We Find Ourselves In

[1]See my argument in Robert Stephen Reid, *Preaching Mark* (St. Louis: Chalice Press, 1999), 163–70.

[2]See Ronald J. Allen, ed., *Patterns of Preaching: A Sermon Sampler* (St. Louis: Chalice Press, 1998), 98–100.

[3]Brian D. McLaren, *The Story We Find Ourselves In: Further Adventures of a New Kind of Christian* (San Francisco: Jossey-Bass, 2003).

[4]Appreciation is offered to Dr. Thomas H. Schattauer of Wartburg Theological Seminary for the use and history of the Christian affirmation *Christos Anesti*.

[5]See Morna D. Hooker, *Endings: Invitations to Discipleship* (Peabody, Mass.: Hendrickson, 2003), 16.

[6]John 14:5, paraphrased.

[7]John 20:25, paraphrased.

[8]John 20:28.

[9]I follow the many scholars who see that John ends his original gospel either here or at the end of 20:21. The remaining verses apparently stem from a later reader who appended another narrative to the gospel. See for instance the notes in *The New Oxford Annotated Bible New Revised Standard Version with the Apocrypha*, 3d ed., ed. M.D. Coogan (Oxford: Oxford University Press, 2001), 181.

[10]See Reid, *Preaching Mark*, 28. The unresolved limerick was created by my friend Alvin Lustie.

Paul's gospel - 21

66. old order has ended because sin has been dealt with.
Mark speaks about Christ coming soon in power because Paul taught that Christ would come soon in power.